Community College

Community College

Is It Right for You?

Susan H. Stafford

WILEY

Wiley Publishing, Inc.

Published by Wiley, Hoboken, NJ
Published simultaneously in Canada

For general information on our other products and services or to obtain technical support please contact our Customer Care Department within the U.S. at 800-762-2974, outside the U.S. at 317-572-3993 or fax 317-572-4002.

Wiley also publishes its books in a variety of electronic formats. Some content that appears in print may not be available in electronic books.

Library of Congress Cataloging-in-Publication data is available from the publisher upon request.

ISBN-13: 978-0-471-77738-0
ISBN-10: 0-471-77738-2

Manufactured in the United States of America

10   9   8   7   6   5   4   3   2   1

Book design by LeAndra Hosier

Cover design by José Almaguer

Page creation by Wiley Publishing, Inc. Composition Services

*To my husband, David, and to my parents,
June and Hubert Huelsebusch*

Acknowledgments

I'm very grateful to many people for helping me learn about and understand the important role that community colleges play in the lives of individuals, their communities, the nation, and beyond. Many of these individuals are quoted throughout the book; others are behind the scenes.

A very special thank-you goes to Dr. George R. Boggs, President and CEO, American Association of Community Colleges, who put community colleges in perspective for me and directed me to many other resources. My gratitude also extends to Dr. Charlene Nunley, President of Montgomery College (Maryland), for kindly opening the doors of this remarkable community college to me, and to her staff members, Steve Simon, Director of Communications, and Elizabeth Homans, Director of Media Relations, who so willingly facilitated many contacts with students, faculty, and administrators at the college. Dr. Stephen M. Curtis, President, Community College of Philadelphia, and Dr. George E. Gabriel, Associate Vice President, Institutional Research, Planning & Assessment and Special Assistant to the President for Marketing, Northern Virginia Community College, offered similar invaluable assistance at their respective institutions. Dr. Pete Mackey, Director of Public Affairs of the Jack Kent Cooke Foundation, and Rod A. Risley, Executive Director of Phi Theta Kappa, the international honor society of community colleges, graciously answered numerous questions and made further referrals to help my interviewing process. Peg Mauzy of Frederick Community College (MD) kindly agreed to an interview and also volunteered to review chapters.

Many friends and colleagues also made this book possible. Author Ceil Cleveland set me on the path of writing this book and cheerfully guided me through the process. To Dr. Mary Ann Castle who read more drafts than seemed humanly possible, thank you with all my heart. Marga C. Fripp, a young woman of great energy and talent who is a graduate of Montgomery College, got the interview ball rolling for me, reviewed chapters, and has my deepest gratitude. Dr. Constance Saulsbery Beck, retired professor of mathematics at Westchester Community College, put me in touch with her former colleagues there and supported my efforts every

Community College: Is It Right for You?

step of the way. Dr. Elizabeth Hull, Dr. Sandra Freels Rosengrant, and Clarice Wilsey generously expanded my contacts at various community colleges. To Ellen Solomon, thank you for sustaining me with your wry good humor and sound advice. Jane Hession gave me perspective by sharing her own experiences as a writer. My thanks also to Rita Siravo for her kind interest in my book.

Thanks also to Grace Freedson, my literary agent, who believed this topic merited attention, and to Greg Tubach and Suzanne Snyder of Wiley Publishing, Inc., for their assistance in seeing the book to completion.

My parents, June and Hubert Huelsebusch, have my love and gratitude for their constant encouragement.

My deepest thanks go to my husband, David, who makes all things possible with his love and support.

Table of Contents

Introduction

> *Community colleges are really the hidden educational jewel of our nation. They offer the stepping stones that set thousands and thousands of people on their way to careers and to further educational opportunities. They are so little recognized, but are a crucial link in our nation's educational system. They are one of our nation's richest resources. We certainly found that to be the case with the quality of services and education offered to our son.*
>
> —Veteran broadcast journalist Judy Woodruff,
> whose disabled son attended Montgomery College (Maryland)

Are you ready for a life-changing event? Do what millions of other people looking for opportunity do—check out your local community college.

Community colleges are affordable and accessible gateways to education that provide opportunities for people to transform their lives. Students of all ages and backgrounds can find a path to fulfill their aspirations through community college. No other type of educational institution in the United States offers so much for so many.

Community colleges are the backbone of this country's educational system and are helping the nation to meet the competitive demands of the 21st century. They are dedicated to helping you achieve your educational, career, and personal goals. Where else could you have the choice of studying to be an emergency medical technician or a Web site designer? Or take a course in photography just for pleasure, or to earn an associate's degree or certificate and start a job as a photographer? If, like many community college students, you have your sights set on transferring to a four-year institution, you've also come to the right place.

Preparing students for further education has always been an important role of community colleges.

If you're thinking of changing careers, community college can help you retool in another field and give you a competitive edge. If you need to brush up on some basic skills or acquire a better command of the English language, you'll find community college is a good place to start. If you're interested in an apprenticeship to be a plumber or electrician, chances are you'll be taking classes at your local community college in addition to your on-the-job training. If you already attend a four-year college, community college can help you tackle some of the required coursework needed to continue your education there.

Community colleges are key players in the economic development of their local areas and regions. They work closely with employers and others in the community to generate new business and to train workers for high-demand jobs. When economic times are tough, they help people refocus their skills and get back to work. They are also community focal points for recreation, cultural and artistic events, sports, and many other activities. Everyone in the community can benefit from some aspect of the local community college.

This could be the year that you decide to start or continue your education, embark on a new career path, improve or acquire new skills for work, or just take a class for fun. Consider community college as an option. No other educational institution in the United States offers so many people so many different paths to a better future and to achieving their goals. Over 11 million people each year go to community college to follow their dreams. You could be one of them.

Let this book be your guide to understanding what community college has to offer and where it can lead you in life. Students of all ages, especially those interested in pursuing a certificate or degree program, will find information that will help you decide whether or not community college is right for you. Parents and high school counselors who are helping recent or soon-to-be graduates look at options will also find this book to be a valuable resource.

Throughout this book, you'll hear from community college students, faculty, and staff who were kind enough to share their thoughts and experiences with me in person, on the phone, or by e-mail. All quotes in this book, unless otherwise noted, are their words of wisdom based on personal interviews. I was consistently struck by their great enthusiasm for community college, as well as their gratitude for the opportunity to be a student there or to work in this educational setting. These individuals' thoughtful comments and perspectives add immeasurably to this book and made writing it a pleasure and an honor for me.

Listen to what they have to say about community college. You could decide it's the right choice for you.

1

Keep Your Options Open: What Can a Community College Do for Me?

> *Community colleges are in the business of changing lives. We are here to meet the broad-based needs of the community. Our doors are open to all members of the community. We base our reputation on these facts and on how we enrich people's lives. It's the best mission you can have in higher education.*

—Dr. Charlene Nunley, President, Montgomery College (Maryland)

Are you a high school student who isn't sure if a four-year college or university is right for you? A working adult who dreams of completing a degree, but hasn't had the time or opportunity? A student who wants to earn a bachelor's degree, but is short on money? An international student seeking an economical way to start your education in the United States? Do you want to upgrade your job skills or start a new career? Do you already have a degree, but still have a thirst for knowledge?

Community college could be the right choice for you.

Because community colleges truly do serve the entire community, they offer a full range of learning opportunities to anyone who wants to pursue more education—whether it leads to a certificate,

1

a degree, a job, or just to more knowledge and enjoyment of life. Community colleges are exciting places because they've got their hands on the pulse of the community and the world of work.

Understanding what community college is and what it can do for you is a smart first step in determining if community college is the right educational pathway for you.

Answer these few short questions to gauge your familiarity with some general features and facts about community colleges.

Test Your Community College Knowledge[1]

1. The highest degree most community colleges offer is:
    a. A bachelor's degree
    b. An associate's degree
    c. A doctoral degree

2. What percentage of community college students attend part-time?
    a. 50 percent
    b. 26 percent
    c. 61 percent

3. The oldest continuously operating public community college was founded in:
    a. 1901
    b. 1854
    c. 1967

4. According to a 2004 American Association of Community Colleges' survey, what is a hot program of study where community college graduates are in high demand?
    a. Registered nurse
    b. Computer technologies
    c. Law enforcement
    d. All of the above

5. What percentage of community college students are the first in their family to attend a postsecondary education institution?

   a. 30 percent
   b. 25 percent
   c. Over 50 percent

Answers: (1) **b.** associate's degree; (2) **c.** 61 percent; (3) **a.** 1901; (4) **d.** all of the above; (5) **c.** over 50 percent.

What Are Community Colleges? Open Doors and Opportunity

Community colleges are accredited two-year institutions of higher education dedicated to serving the educational and workforce needs of their local communities. They are often called "the people's college" because of their philosophy that anyone can benefit from a college education. Community colleges welcome a diverse population of women and men of all ages, abilities, races and ethnicities, backgrounds, nationalities, and degrees of academic preparation. Open admission policies, low tuition rates, flexible schedules, and convenient locations make them easily accessible to the public.

> *"Community college is the American ideal of democracy in action in education."*
>
> —Rob Jenkins, Associate Professor of English and Director of The Writers Institute, Georgia Perimeter College (Georgia)

Some community colleges are large, urban institutions with several campuses serving thousands of students; others are in rural settings with small student populations; some serve suburban communities on the fringes of mid-sized or large cities or towns. Most community colleges are public; others are independent or private. They are all dedicated to teaching and learning, open access, and quality education for everyone.

At community college, you can train for some of the fastest growing jobs in the economy, or follow a course of study that will allow you to transfer into a bachelor's degree program at a four-year institution. You can also take courses just for pleasure or to improve your work skills.

AREAS OF EDUCATION

Most community colleges offer a comprehensive range of programs in the following general areas of education:

✓ **Basic skills education** (sometimes called developmental or remedial education) in reading, writing, mathematics, and English language skills to prepare you for college-level academics, if needed, before you start a particular course of study. Most of these courses do not carry any college credit; that is, they do not count toward a certificate or degree.

✓ **Academic preparation for transfer** (movement) to an upper division (junior/senior year) college or four-year institution to study for a bachelor's (baccalaureate) degree. Your first two years of general education courses at community college may count toward your four-year degree if you decide to transfer.

✓ **Vocational and technical education** (training in a skilled trade or technology) to prepare you for direct entry into the workplace with a certificate or degree. Transfer to a four-year institution is also a possibility in some programs; sometimes additional coursework is required.

✓ **Continuing education and workforce development,** ranging from a wide variety of courses designed for personal enrichment to programs that respond to the specific needs of business and industry for skilled workers. Many of these courses are non-credit and do not lead to a certificate or degree.

See Chapter 3 for more information about educational opportunities at community colleges.

SOME BACKGROUND ON COMMUNITY COLLEGES

Each year, community colleges help build an educated and skilled workforce in the communities they serve. They give millions of individuals like you a first or next step up their personal ladders of success. And, they've been doing this job in local communities, right where you live, for over a hundred years.

Here are some facts you may not know about community colleges.

✓ As of 2004, the American Association of Community Colleges says there are 1,158 community colleges in the United States, of which 979 are public, 148 are private, and 31 are tribal.[2]

✓ Community colleges will serve nearly 12 million students this year—a projected 6.67 million undergraduates[3] plus another 5 million students in non-credit courses that are mainly short-term job training.[4]

> **FAST FACT:** In 2005, 45 percent of all undergraduates in the United States were enrolled in two-year degree-granting post-secondary institutions.[5]

Because community colleges play such an important role in higher education and one might soon play an important role in your life, you should know a little about how they began and about their contributions.

Community colleges are one of America's most successful education stories. Junior colleges, as community colleges were first known, initially emphasized general liberal arts studies and prepared students to transfer to four-year (senior) colleges and universities. And, they did this in the neighborhoods and communities where the students lived and at an affordable cost, features that were innovative for the time. Founded in 1901, Joliet Junior College in Illinois is the oldest public community college in the country.

Another hallmark of community colleges is their ability to respond rapidly to the changing demands and conditions of the times. They added job training programs during the Depression, educated returning soldiers from World War II for re-entry into the workforce, and significantly expanded facilities and programs in the 1960s as the economy and population grew. More recently, community colleges have answered the needs of students for flexible schedules, basic skills (developmental) education, new life-long learning opportunities, English as a second language, distance learning, and more. As new technologies emerge, business and industry turn first to community colleges to train the workforce.

Community colleges serve their communities in many other ways. They generate millions of dollars in revenue, help train new leadership, work with community partners to remedy social and economic problems, and are often the vibrant core of athletic, cultural, and artistic life for the community. Most important, they open the door to new opportunities, choices, and futures for people like you each year.[6]

FAST FACT: Other countries worldwide have adapted the American community college model to make education more accessible to their own citizens and to strengthen their workforces.[7]

Community Colleges and Four-Year Institutions

Community colleges and four-year colleges and universities are institutions of higher education. Although they all play important roles in educating students and helping people get their start in life, it helps to keep their basic differences in mind as you think about which may be better for you.

The table below sets out major aspects of each type of institution. You'll find more detailed information about community college programs, how to select a community college, and details about admissions in subsequent chapters.

Comparing Types of Colleges

Community College	Four-Year Private or Public Institution
Many community colleges have open admissions policies, meaning that anyone who can benefit is welcome to attend. There are usually minimal qualifications for admission to degree and certificate programs; however, some programs—especially in the allied health sciences—are highly selective, have rigorous admissions criteria, and accept only a small number of students each year.	Four-year colleges and universities vary in their degrees of selectivity and some do have open admissions policies. Selection is most often based on competitive factors including stan-dardized test scores, such as the SAT and ACT, high school grade point average and coursework, letters of recommendation, and admissions essays. A high school diploma or high school equivalency certificate (GED) is gen-erally required in order for an applicant to be admitted.
You will need a high school diploma or a high school equivalency certificate based on the General Educational Development (GED) test to take courses for credit. Many non-credit courses are generally open to anyone who wants to enroll.	
Students take assessment and placement tests to determine their appropriate class level. Basic skills or developmental courses, plus English language classes, may be required prior to enrollment in college-level courses for credit.	

continued

Comparing Types of Colleges (continued)

Community College	Four-Year Private or Public Institution
The community college student body is often described as "non-traditional," referring to independent, older adults who are entering college for the first time or returning after some time. "Traditional" college-age students (18–22 years old) entering directly from high school are increasing in numbers, especially as full-time students in day programs.	Many students in baccalaureate programs start right out of high school and fall into the traditional college-age range of 18–22 years.
Most students are in-state residents from the local area; some foreign-born students also attend.	Students come from across the country and around the world.
The majority of students attend part time (less than 12 credit hours per semester).	Most students attend on a full-time basis.
Most community colleges offer a comprehensive curriculum (course of study) that focuses mainly on liberal arts and sciences, *plus* vocational and technical training for direct entry into the workforce, an option that most four-year institutions do not offer. Continuing education and workforce development programs are integral to community colleges' mission to meet local needs.	The undergraduate curriculum (course of study) focuses mainly on liberal arts and sciences, preparation for professional degrees such as law or medicine, and preparation for other graduate level education. Many four-year institutions also offer continuing education and workforce training programs.

Community College	Four-Year Private or Public Institution
An associate's degree is usually the highest degree awarded; however, a few states—Florida, Arkansas, Utah—have begun to allow community colleges to offer a bachelor's (baccalaureate) degree. Most degree programs can be completed in 2 years of full-time attendance. Certificate programs typically take a year or less to complete if you go full time.	All four-year colleges and universities offer a bachelor's (baccalaureate) degree as the highest undergraduate degree. Some also offer an associate's degree. The bachelor's degree typically takes 4 to 6 years to complete.
Community colleges are mainly geared to commuters; however, about 20 percent of community colleges do offer a more traditional college experience with on-campus housing available to students.[8]	Most four-year institutions are geared to full-time, residential students with on-campus housing in dormitories widely available (although they may also have a commuter population).
Faculty members are mainly focused on teaching as their primary responsibility; many colleges require faculty to have master's degrees and there are a growing number who also hold doctorates.	Faculty members' focus is divided among teaching, research, and publication; there is a higher percentage of faculty with doctorates than in community colleges.

continued

Comparing Types of Colleges (continued)	
Community College	**Four-Year Private or Public Institution**
Class size averages between 25 and 40 students. Classes are taught by full-time or part-time (adjunct) faculty.	Although average class size varies, many lower-division (freshman and sophomore) classes, especially lecture classes, can be very large and are often taught by graduate teaching assistants.
Tuition for community colleges is affordable.	Tuition costs at public institutions are usually at least twice that of community colleges and often more at a private institution.

Some Reasons to Consider Community College

Community colleges are rapidly becoming the "college of choice" for many recent high school graduates, as well as older students. Why? Because today's students want and need an accessible and flexible high-quality education at an affordable price. Community colleges offer just that.

Community college isn't the right choice for everyone, but there may be one or more good reasons why community college might be the right place for you. Consider the following benefits:

✓ **It's a great bargain.** You can't beat the low cost of community college. A public community college's annual tuition and fees are about half those of public four-year colleges and less than 10–15 percent of those of private four-year institutions.

SNAPSHOT: Igor Levine, a 2005 graduate of Montgomery College (Maryland) who is now studying economics and political science at Columbia University, says, "Going to community college made economic sense to me. I came here when I was 14 from Moscow to play the professional tennis circuit. I had what is the equivalent of a high school diploma. As I grew older, however, I realized I needed more education to succeed, but four-year college here is expensive. I knew I could save a lot of money by going to community college so I enrolled. I've been fortunate because I got into the the College's Macklin Business Institute honors program with a scholarship. My grades and extracurricular activities got me into Columbia."

If you live at home, you can also save money on room and board. Financial aid can help you graduate with no or low debt. If you want to go on to four-year college, but don't have the money yet, attending a community college can help you cut back on expenses and earn transferable college credits until you have the funds to make the switch.

FAST FACT: The College Board reports that the average published tuition and fees for 2005–2006 is $2,191 for public two-year colleges, $5,491 for public four-year colleges and universities, and $21,235 for private nonprofit four-year colleges.[9]

✓ **You can get in and get started.** So your grades aren't or weren't so great, or your SAT or ACT scores weren't stellar. The door to college hasn't been slammed in your face. Community college gives you a chance at a college education.

Rather than delay your education, take advantage of community college's open admissions policy and get started. Build a stronger academic record that can help you transfer to a four-year college, or choose a more direct route to a career. The longer you wait, the longer before you achieve your goals.

✓ **You can stay close to home.** Community colleges are usually located where you live or are usually within easy reach. Many of them have a main campus and branch campuses so that you have easy and convenient access to their services without living on campus.

> *"I could have attended a four-year institution first, but I chose Montgomery College because of its excellent reputation, affordable cost, and closeness to home. I saved enough money in two years to ensure that my last two years at Rutgers University wouldn't be a financial burden. I got an excellent education and had opportunities I might not have had as a freshman or sophomore at a four-year school, including a two-week study-abroad program at Cambridge University."*
> —Judith Martinez, Montgomery College (Maryland), Class of 2004

✓ **You can get a flexible schedule.** You can find a schedule of courses that fits into your personal schedule. Community colleges are geared to students who work full time or part time and who have families and other commitments. They are open days, evenings, and weekends, and you can study part time or full time. In addition, distance learning courses—online, video, television—offer students an alternative means of taking coursework that is often adjustable to any schedule.

✓ **You can get help with the basics.** Community colleges are focused on your success. If you need additional help with the basics—writing, reading, mathematics, science, study skills—they will help you gain or strengthen these skills through basic developmental skills classes. So if you missed out on the basics in high school or have forgotten some of them because you've been out of school for a while, you'll have an opportunity to catch up before you plunge into college-level classes. The aim is to help you be successful in your coursework.

Most community colleges also have special programs and services for students who are at risk academically. If English is not your first language, you'll also be in the right place, as there are special programs to help you.

✓ **You can be the center of attention.** Community colleges generally offer smaller classes and more individual student attention than many four-year colleges. Although faculty members do conduct research and publish, their main focus is on teaching you.

Small class size and more personal attention help many students gain confidence and thrive academically. Tutoring, learning resource centers, and many forms of assistance are also available to help you succeed.

✓ **You can test-drive the college experience.** You may be undecided about whether or not you are ready for college, or if you even want to go to college. A two-year experience can help you gain the skills and confidence to go on to four-year schools. Or, it can help you decide you'd rather learn a technical skill and start your career. Either way, you always have the option to continue your education in the future.

✓ **You can take time to adjust.** Making the change from high school to college is a big adjustment. Sometimes, it's just too much to handle all at once. High school students who enroll in four-year institutions often find that they get sidetracked by campus social life, are homesick, or simply don't do well in their studies. Sometimes, life at the college or university that you chose just isn't what you expected.

If you're not ready to be on your own, community college is a great option. You can continue to live at home, get your feet wet at college, and focus on your studies. Community college can be an excellent bridge between high school and a four-year institution.

SNAPSHOT: Whitney Gentile enrolled in a state university in Texas, but found that the experience of a large campus wasn't what she anticipated. "I discovered that I couldn't just major in theater arts, which was what I wanted to do. Instead, I had to take a major in each of four different areas: dance, music, theater, art. I was exhausted trying to meet all the requirements. It was also hard being 18 and moving away from everything I knew even though I had some friends from home on campus. I've been working for a while and deciding what to do. I'm going to enroll in my local community college—Montgomery Community College (Texas). I plan to take some of my core courses before enrolling in another four-year school, probably to major in French. Going to community college will help me get refocused and not lose too much time."

✓ **You can explore your options.** Community colleges offer a broad range of vocational and technical studies, as well as liberal arts and science coursework.

Through the college's career center, academic counseling, and other support services, you can explore what it takes to jump-start a career in fields as varied as accounting, culinary arts, criminal justice, nursing, or computer technology. You can also take courses without credit to see if a certain field is right for you, or to improve your readiness to enter the world of work. You can even enroll in a vocational or technical course such as automotive technology at the same time you're studying art, history, or another subject in a general studies or liberal arts and science track.

✓ **You can chart a pathway to a four-year institution of your choice.** Preparing students to transfer to a four-year institution is one of the original purposes of community college. Many four-year colleges and community colleges, especially those in the same state, have agreements to accept credits from community colleges toward the baccalaureate degree. Many state educational systems give first priority to transfer students from in-state community colleges to their four-year institutions. High-achieving students from community colleges are also accepted at prestigious four-year institutions such as Harvard University, Stanford University, and Smith College. See Chapter 10 for more information about the transfer process and requirements.

FAST FACT: A long-term study of students first enrolled in public two-year institutions in 1995–1996 showed that 9 out of 10 enrolled with the intention of obtaining a formal credential (such as a certificate or degree) or of transferring to a four-year institution.[10]

✓ **You can enter the workforce faster with a career-oriented degree.** Community colleges offer many programs leading directly to a career. You can earn a two-year associate's degree or enter a shorter-term certificate program (usually a year or less) that offers intensive training in a specialized field. These programs are often not available at four-year institutions.

Moreover, studies show repeatedly that education translates into greater earnings over your lifetime. Individuals with an associate's degree or technical and vocational certificates consistently earn more than those who have only a high school diploma. The more education you have, the greater your earning potential.

FAST FACT: Graduates with an associate's degree can expect to earn more than $1.6 million in their lifetimes, about $400,000 more than someone with only a high school diploma.[11]

✓ **You can connect with employers.** Community colleges are networked with your potential employers. They know what fields are "hot" and what skills the market demands because they ask employers what they need. Community colleges often revise their coursework based on advice from employers.

Community colleges also offer internships, cooperative education opportunities, and community service learning programs that can give you a competitive edge in finding a job after you graduate or in getting accepted by a four-year college or university.

✓ **You can stay competitive in your field or start a new career.** Community colleges offer a great opportunity for you to upgrade skills to help you in your current job, or to learn new ones that will help you find a new position in the same or a different field. Many employers partner with community colleges to provide employees with specific training to keep them current with changes in their fields. Some employers will pay for job-related coursework.

✓ **You can expand your mind.** Community colleges are great places to explore a subject just for the fun of learning. Many adults enroll in continuing education courses to pursue a personal interest, such as learning a language or getting a grip on personal finances. Sometimes, this experience can motivate you to enroll in an academic or vocational program and earn a certificate or degree, or go on to a four-year school.

Reality Check: Is Community College Right for Me?

Here are some questions to ask yourself to help you determine if your next step should be community college. Your personal circumstances, grades, vocational and career interests, and finances are all factors that will enter into your decision.

If You're Just Graduating from High School

❑ Could I use some help and time to strengthen my basic skills—writing, reading, math, and science—and my academic record?

❑ Am I interested in starting a career in a short period of time? Do I want to explore vocational and technical career options?

❑ Am I ready to be on my own at college living away from my family and friends?

❑ Do I need some time to decide what I want to do before making a commitment to a four-year institution?

❑ Can I afford a four-year college at this time?

If You're an Adult Considering Community College

❑ Can I afford to put off my education any longer?

❑ Do I want to continue in the same career or job, or am I ready for something new?

❑ Could I improve my current or future job situation by updating my skills?

❑ Will a smaller, more intimate environment help me be successful in the classroom?

❑ Do I need a flexible schedule so that I can juggle the demands of work, family, and community while attending college?

Find Out More

✦ Check out the excellent Web site of the American Association of Community Colleges (www.aacc.nche.edu). You'll find a wealth of information about community colleges and their history, as well as a community college locator and advice for parents and students.

✦ The College Board Web site (www.collegeboard.com) is a comprehensive site for information about community colleges, as well as four-year institutions.

✦ *Peterson's Two-Year Colleges* (Thomson's Peterson), an annual guide, plus their Web site (www.petersons.com), offer advice for high school adult students who want to go to community colleges, career colleges, and for-profit colleges, plus specific information about these colleges such as location, number of students, types of degrees and majors offered, and more.

2

Know Your Classmates: Who Goes to Community College?

> *One of the best features of community colleges is that they are inclusive. Community colleges do not seek to exclude anyone, and we see potential in all of our students. All types of students can benefit from a community college experience.*
>
> —Dr. Stephen M. Curtis, President,
> Community College of Philadelphia (Pennsylvania)

There's no one answer to the question of who goes to community college because community colleges have traditionally opened their doors to everyone who wants to improve themselves by learning. As education becomes more and more important to getting ahead, community colleges strive to meet the needs of an increasingly diverse population of students of all ages, backgrounds, educational goals, and levels of academic preparation.

This chapter gives you some insight into who goes to community college and who might be your future classmates. Of course, where you live determines just how diverse the student body will be at your local college; but no matter what, you'll have the opportunity to meet a broad spectrum of people from your community and beyond.

A Kaleidoscope of Diversity

Although there is no one "typical" community college student, a 2005 survey of over 133,000 students across the country showed some characteristics that many community college students share.[1]

Community college students tend to be older than what is often considered to be a typical college-age student (18–22 years old). Most students are working, are enrolled part time, and have other significant responsibilities, such as children or other family commitments.

Community colleges serve a racially and ethnically diverse student population. Many community college students come from low-income families and are often the first members of their families to attend college.

Some students entering community college have been well-prepared to continue their education after high school, but many have not. Other community college students have already earned a higher education degree such as a certificate, associate's, or bachelor's degree, or even a graduate degree.

Many students also face challenges and obstacles to their success because of life circumstances and competing demands on their time.

DIVERSITY IN AGE AND LIFE EXPERIENCE

Keep in mind that community college is one place where age doesn't matter. Community colleges pride themselves on being centers of lifelong learning opportunities and often offer services and programs for all age groups, from pre-kindergarten tots to senior citizens.

Traditional-Age Students

If you're a high school student considering community college, you'll find plenty of students in your age group. In fact, you are one of the fastest growing segments of the community college population. As of 2001, 42 percent of community college students were under the age of 22, representing an increase of almost 10 percent over the last decade.[2]

Although some students in this age range live at home and are dependent on their parents, many work part time. Some even have children or other family responsibilities, or are financially independent of their parents. Many traditional-age students are eager to get started on a career or enter with the intention of transferring to a four-year college after a year or two.

Amanda Alkins, who is the first person in her immediate family to attend college, enrolled in the Community College of Philadelphia right out of high school. She lives at home but is financing her studies with scholarships, loans, work, and some help from her parents. In two years, she has completed the coursework necessary to enter the nursing program, met its rigorous requirements, and is on her way to earning a two-year associate's degree to become a registered nurse.

Travis Huelsebusch, now a 22-year-old pilot, started out as a full-time student in an aviation maintenance technology program at Cincinnati State Technical and Community College. Through work, the military, and help from his parents, he is paying for his education. He intends to become a fighter pilot in the United States Air Force after transferring to a regional branch of Embry-Riddle Aeronautical University for his bachelor's degree.

Community college could also be the perfect place for you to get your start in life if you're a traditional-age student.

Nontraditional-Age Students

If you're thinking "I'm too old to go back to college," remember that the average age of a community college student is 29![3] And, you're in the majority. In fact, about 60 percent of community college students are over the age of 22 and 15 percent are over age 40.[4]

Most nontraditional-age students are financially independent adults who work full or part time and juggle family and community responsibilities while attending college. Because of these responsibilities, they are often part-time students who attend evening or weekend classes.

> *"I started out at a four-year college and got sidetracked. Instead of studying, I got too involved in my social life and athletics. Consequently, I dropped out. When I was ready to go back, I was 26 and more mature. I could appreciate the value of my education. I enrolled in community college and [was] taken under the wing of a faculty member who really helped me out. I went on to get a master's degree and a PhD in educational administration with a specialization in community college leadership."*
>
> —Dr. Marvin Bright, Dean of Students, Community College of Philadelphia

As a nontraditional-age student, the reasons you would seek out a community college education are varied. You may want to go to community college because you never had a chance to attend college earlier in life, or left college before completing a degree. Aimee Tootsey, mother of two teenage daughters, returned to college at age 37 because she always regretted not having a college degree. She enrolled at Montgomery College (Maryland), found she had a gift for learning, and was accepted into the Millennium Scholars program—a selective honors program that is open to all students, but is especially designed for part-time students with classes in the evening and on weekends at Montgomery's Germantown campus. She is currently studying history at Hood College where she is on a full scholarship.

Other returning adults come back to upgrade their work skills or to retool for a new career. Roy R. Gordon, a postal service executive in his forties and holder of six technology patents, started college several times, but never completed a degree. He decided to prepare himself for a new career in business or finance after he retires by attending Montgomery College while working full time. Like Aimee Tootsey, he too participated in the Millennium Scholars honors program. After graduating in the spring of 2005 with honors and as a member of the Phi Theta Kappa honor society, he received a transfer scholarship to attend the University of Maryland University College (UMUC).

Many nontraditional-age students also come to community college to take courses for the pleasure of learning, to earn a high school equivalency degree, to learn English, to acquire new skills for work, or to keep abreast of new technology. When Dr. Norman Barr, a prominent ear, nose, and throat physician, decided he needed to upgrade his computer skills, he enrolled in continuing education courses at a convenient local campus of Northern Virginia Community College.

TIP: If you haven't been in school for a while or are entering college for the first time, community college can be the best place to start. Here are some reasons:

- ✓ The small class environment can ease your transition back into school.

- ✓ You may be able to receive some credit for your life experience that can count toward your degree.

- ✓ Many colleges have special programs and offices for returning adult students.

DIVERSITY IN GENDER, RACE, AND ETHNICITY

Community colleges thrive on the diversity of their student bodies, reflecting their commitment to helping people from all sectors of society to advance.

If you live in a large city or suburban area, you will certainly be in classes with people from many different cultural, racial, ethnic, social, and economic backgrounds. Even in rural areas, there can be a surprising diversity, including students from other countries.

Approximately 33 percent of community college students come from minority backgrounds (see chart below). As the nation's immigrant population grows, more and more students come from families who recently settled in the United States. Community college offers these students and their families a way to gain English language skills as needed, and to benefit from our educational system.

For many students with low incomes, community college is the most affordable way to gain a toehold in higher education. Many students from impoverished circumstances have to overcome considerable challenges to succeed. Alex San Pedro, for example, faced homelessness as a teenager on the streets of San Francisco and battled alcoholism in his twenties before finding his way to Lane Community College (Oregon), where he found art was his passion. He is now studying art at Pratt Institute in New York City.

Here are a few more facts about the diversity of community college students that you should keep in mind.

Community College Student Population[5]

By gender and part-time/full-time status:

58% of all students enrolled are women; 42% are men.

61% of all students attend part time; 39% attend full time.

38.4% of students of all ages attending in 2003–2004 worked part time and 41.6% worked full time. Only 20% in all age groups did not work while they attended college.

By race and ethnicity:

59% White (non-Hispanic)

13.8% Hispanic

| 12.5% African-American |
| 6.25% Asian/Pacific Islander |
| 2.09% American Indian/Alaska Native |
| (5.5% race unknown; 0.15% nonresident alien) |

You'll also find that the world comes to you, as community colleges of all sizes and geographic locations attract international students, as well as foreign-born students already living in the United States. Montgomery College, which has been mentioned previously, is a large suburban community college near Washington, D.C., with students from 170 nations—one of the most diverse student bodies in the country!

According to Dr. George R. Boggs, President and CEO of the American Association of Community Colleges, "International students add an important dimension to community college life. We have to prepare students for an increasingly global society and economy. Having international students at community colleges promotes cultural exchange and understanding."

With the exception of international students and some students from outside your district or state, most students will come from the local area served by the college, so members of the community will be your classmates.

FAST FACT: 95.5 percent of undergraduate students in public community college attended in their home state at an average distance of 33 miles from home.[6]

DIVERSITY IN ACADEMIC BACKGROUND

Community colleges offer students of all levels of academic experience and achievement the opportunity to learn more. Some students will be attending college for the first time. Others, as mentioned earlier in this chapter, may already have some experience with college studies.

Many students, like Musa Saquee, a high school graduate in his 20s and a refugee from Sierra Leone, will need to take some basic skills and language courses before being admitted to college-level coursework. He is studying at Gwinett Technical College (Georgia) where he hopes to enter the radiologic technician program.

Some students you'll meet will be academically high-achieving students who are taking honors courses or even high school students who are enrolled in both high school and college. Others will already have earned a certificate or degree from community college or a four-year institution. Some may even have an advanced degree such as a master's degree or PhD. Students with degrees come back for many reasons: they're seeking a new career, are taking a short-term course for work reasons, or are coming back just for the pleasure of learning something new.

Other students will be enrolled in four-year institutions and studying for their bachelor's or a higher degree. They will be taking a course or two at community college to meet some of the requirements at the college they regularly attend. Jane Hession, an architectural historian, for instance, needed to take physics and calculus for her professional graduate degree in architecture at the University of Minnesota. She chose to take the courses at nearby Normandale Community College instead because it was close to home.

FAST FACT: 28 percent of community colleges' non-credit students have a bachelor's degree or higher, while over a quarter of part-time community college students enrolled for credit have some form of postsecondary [after high school] education.[7]

In summary, no matter what your age, background, personal history, level of academic preparation, or life circumstance, community college has a place for you. Just like the diverse group of students mentioned above, you too can find the educational opportunity you need at community college.

Well-Known People Who Have Attended Community College

Famous people from many walks of life, including many of the country's most successful and respected business leaders, government officials, entertainers, scientists, and sports figures, have attended community college. You'll be in good company if you decide to go.

Bonnie Blair
Olympic Speedskater
Parkland College, IL

Rita Mae Brown
Author
Broward Community College, FL

Richard Carmona, M.D.
U.S. Surgeon General
Bronx Community College, NY

Eileen Collins
Astronaut and Commander of the Space Shuttle
Corning Community College, NY

Clint Eastwood
Academy Award-Winning Actor and Director
Los Angeles Community College, CA

Calvin Klein
Fashion Designer
Fashion Institute of Technology, NY

Jim Lehrer
Broadcast Journalist
MacNeil/Lehrer News Hour
Victoria College, TX

H. Ross Perot
Billionaire Computer Executive and 1992 Presidential Candidate
Texarkana Junior College, TX

Gaddi Vasquez
Director, Peace Corps
Santa Ana College, CA

J. Craig Ventor
Entrepreneur and Scientist Who First Mapped the Human Genome
College of San Mateo, CA

Now that you've seen how community college accommodates a rich diversity of students, you will learn about what educational paths and programs of study are available to you in the next chapter.

Find Out More

✦ Check the American Association of Community College's Web site, www.aacc.nche.edu, for more information about diversity among community college students and for a more complete list of famous people who have attended community college.

✦ The Community College Survey of Student Engagement (CCSSE) is an annual national-level survey of community college students. The Web site, www.ccsse.org, provides excellent information about survey results, challenges facing community college students, profiles of students, plus online video interviews with community college students.

Know the Choices: What Can I Study?

For purposes of instruction, community colleges are one of the most important and exciting places in America right now. They're keeping the educational door open for many people who, because of money, work, family responsibilities, or other reasons, might not have the initial option of attending a four-year college. They can, however, get a good start at community college and go to work or go on for more education. It's surprising, but many people don't realize what assets their local community colleges really are and the opportunities they offer.

—James Carville, Political Strategist, Author, and Instructor for "Issues in American Politics" at Northern Virginia Community College, Fall 2005.

Community colleges are great places to start the next phase of your education because they offer so many options, both in courses of study and paths to achieve your goals.

Just look at any community college catalog or at the programs listed at the college's Web site. You'll find a wide choice of subjects to study, from accounting to computer technology, to nursing, to automotive mechanics, to personal finances. Remember that community colleges are geared to responding to the needs of the local and national economies, so you'll find coursework related to filling jobs in areas of high demand. Obviously, not every course of study is available at every community college, but you should be able to find a program that suits your needs and interests.

According to a recent study by the American Association of Community Colleges,[1] the top five fields of study, or "hot" programs where community college graduates are in high demand, are:

✓ allied health such as registered nursing, licensed practical nursing, and radiologic technology.

✓ information technologies such as computer technologies, networking, and graphic design.

✓ industrial skilled trades such as automotive technology, construction, welding, and trucking.

✓ business such as general business, paralegal studies, and accounting.

✓ public services such as law enforcement, emergency medical services, and homeland security.

Community colleges are flexible and responsive to local and national needs so they can add programs to meet new concerns, such as homeland security, and can discontinue those with low enrollment or declining demand from business and industry. You'll want to remember this as you begin your studies.

FAST FACT: Community colleges train over 50 percent of new nurses and about 85 percent of first-responders such as firefighters, law enforcement officers, and emergency medical technicians.[2]

Options! Options! Options!
Paths to Achieve Your Goals

Whether your goal is to earn a vocational or technical degree and jump into the workforce as quickly as possible or begin working toward a bachelor's degree or beyond, you will be able to start your journey at a community college. You'll also have opportunities for shorter-term study through non-credit continuing education and workforce development programs.

- ✓ **Path 1: Preparing for college-level courses.** If you need help with the basics, as many students do, you'll be able to start out in courses that will prepare you for college-level classes.

- ✓ **Path 2: Preparing for transfer**. If you know you want to go on to a four-year institution, you can plan your studies in a transfer program so that you can continue to pursue a bachelor's degree. You can, of course, also decide to enter the workforce.

- ✓ **Path 3: Preparing for the world of work**. If you've already got your sights set on entering the job market, you can focus on a more career-oriented program in a vocational or technical program. Short-term certificate programs can also jumpstart your entry into the job market. (You can also choose to transfer to a four-year institution, but that's not the main purpose of this coursework—see below).

- ✓ **Path 4: Learning for life and work.** If you start off taking non-credit courses in continuing education and workforce development programs for personal enrichment, general knowledge, or to improve your work skills, you may be motivated to enroll in a degree or certificate program.

PATH 1. PREPARING FOR COLLEGE-LEVEL COURSES

If you need assistance with basic skills such as reading, writing, English composition, mathematics, science, or English as a Second Language, as many new students do, you'll be required to take some of these courses *before* enrolling in college-level courses.

Terms You Should Know:

✓ **Certificate:** An award for the completion of a short-term, for-credit, vocational or technical program of study.

✓ **Credit Courses:** Courses that earn academic credit and count toward a degree or certificate.

✓ **Curriculum:** A program of studies.

✓ **Degree:** An award for the successful completion of a required course of study.

✓ **Liberal Arts:** A course of study that develops general knowledge and reasoning ability for a well-rounded education. Language, history, and literature are examples of the liberal arts.

✓ **Major:** A focused area of study, such as history, biology, nursing, or automotive technology, in which you take many courses to gain specialized knowledge.

✓ **Non-Credit Courses:** Courses that do not earn academic credit and that do not count toward a for-credit degree or certificate.

✓ **Technical Program:** A program that gives you special and usually practical knowledge in a mechanical or scientific subject, such as aviation mechanics or computer technology.

✓ **Transfer Program:** A two-year curriculum designed for you to earn credits that will be accepted by a four-year institution.

✓ **Vocational Program:** A program that gives you training in a specific occupation, such as interior design, or a particular skill or trade, such as building construction.

Community colleges offer basic skills coursework, also called developmental education, plus learning resource centers and specially trained staff who will help you prepare to enroll and succeed in regular college-level coursework. If you're a returning adult, the department of continuing education can also be a way to catch up on basic skills, take English-as-a-Second Language courses, or complete your high school diploma or GED (usually necessary to be admitted to the college to take for-credit courses).

Usually, these types of basic skills courses are non-credit courses; that is, they do not count toward the number of credits you need for a degree or certificate. If you need this type of instruction, even if it's only one or two courses, it will be your first step toward enrolling in college-level courses and earning a degree or a certificate.

Once you pass the necessary requirements, you'll be prepared to follow whatever path you choose to a career or to additional education at a four-year institution.

PATH 2. PREPARING FOR TRANSFER

Preparing students to transfer to a four-year institution is one of the most important jobs of community colleges. Many, if not most, community colleges have transfer agreements called *articulation agreements* with four-year institutions. These agreements allow course credit earned at community college to be accepted or transferred and applied to a bachelor's degree at a four-year institution. (See Chapter 10 for more information about transferring.)

Transfer programs allow you to follow a two-year course of study designed to prepare you to move into a bachelor's degree program at a four-year institution. The coursework you take for your degree will be similar to courses that you would take in the first two years of study at a four-year institution to earn your bachelor's degree.

You'll be able to earn an Associate's degree in Arts (AA) or an Associate's degree in Science (AS). These degrees usually require a minimum of 60 hours of credit. If you are able to attend full time, ideally, this degree will take two years to complete. Because many community college students attend part time, it can obviously take longer.

You can select a broad field such as liberal arts or education, or declare a major (special area of study) in a specific field such as history or biology. Some community colleges have pre-professional programs that will prepare you for further study at a four-year school (and beyond), with an eye to entering professions such as architecture, dentistry, engineering, law, pharmacy, medicine, and optometry.

> *"Community college is about options and new chances. Students who start out in a vocational or technical program may decide that they want to go on to a four-year institution for a bachelor's degree. Other times, students come with the intention of transferring to a four-year institution and find they're most interested in a vocational or technical area and getting a job. At community college you can gain confidence in your academic skills, test out both areas, and decide which one's right for you."*
>
> —Dennis L. Bailey-Fougnier,
> Associate Dean of Student Development,
> Portland Community College (Oregon)

If you choose this path, with careful planning, your program of study will allow you to meet the admissions criteria set by four-year colleges and to transfer all or most of the credits that you took at community college.

Associate in Arts (AA)

The Associate in Arts (AA) degree is designed specifically for students who want to transfer into an upper division (junior/senior year) at a four-year institution to complete a bachelor's degree.

Your coursework for this degree gives you a broad base of knowledge in the liberal arts and sciences (liberal arts include the social sciences [such as anthropology, psychology, and sociology], humanities [art, theater, and music], the biological and physical sciences, and mathematics) instead of focusing on the skills and knowledge for immediate entry into the workforce. You'll still be preparing yourself for a job if you get this degree; it's just that your immediate intention is to transfer to a four-year institution to complete a bachelor's degree.

An AA degree in communications arts will help you prepare for work in public relations, journalism, and publishing, or to continue in a similar field at a four-year institution. Many students who intend to be teachers receive their AA degrees and then pursue a bachelor's degree in education and receive their teaching certificates. You could earn an AA in business to prepare for further study in accounting or finance at a four-year school.

Some colleges offer specific or special transfer degrees. For example, the Associate of Arts Transfer degree at Oregon community colleges allows you to take coursework in several disciplines and, when completed, guarantees you junior standing at Portland State University and other educational institutions in Oregon. The Teacher Education Transfer Program at Montgomery College (Maryland) offers an Associate of Arts in Teaching (AAT) that prepares students to transfer to an early childhood education program at a four-year college or university in the state of Maryland. Be sure to check with your college to see the full range of associate degrees offered.

TIP: If you're planning to transfer to a four-year institution for your bachelor's degree, you don't necessarily have to complete the requirements for an associate's degree. You could just earn your credits and transfer. Getting the degree, however, gives you an academic credential that's yours forever. It shows that you can complete a program of study, looks good on your resumé, and can be helpful on a job application. And, if for some reason, life interferes, and you don't complete the bachelor's degree, you still have your associate's degree from community college as an academic credential.

Associate in Science (AS)

The Associate in Science (AS) degree is similar to the Associate in Arts, but—as its title implies—includes more science and mathematics coursework. It also enables you to transfer to an upper division or four-year college to obtain a Bachelor of Science degree in a related field. Majors in this type of program include subjects such as biology, chemistry, geology, or forestry.

An AS in engineering science, for example, gives you the foundation for earning a bachelor's degree in engineering and developing a career in chemical, aerospace, or mechanical engineering. An AS degree in computer science could help you gain an entry-level job in the field, or go on to a four-year institution and become a software programmer or systems analyst.

Again, you can also opt to enter the job market directly with an AS degree in many fields.

> **FAST FACT:** A transfer program is often called a 2 + 2 program because you spend two years at community college followed by two years at a four-year institution to earn your bachelor's degree.

Note: Because some students decide to transfer before earning their associate's degree, some colleges have begun to offer a transfer studies certificate. Montgomery College, for instance, offers this option to students to facilitate their transfer to in-state and out-of-state colleges. Students can design their coursework to meet the four-year institution's requirements and earn the transfer studies certificate when they have 30 appropriate credits.

PATH 3. PREPARING FOR THE WORLD OF WORK: VOCATIONAL/TECHNICAL PROGRAMS

Most community colleges offer (and some specialize in) vocational and technical training that allows you to enter employment directly. You can follow a course of study leading to a two-year associate's degree or enter a certificate program if you prefer a shorter program of study.

These programs usually require specialized courses in fields such as business, health occupations, trade and industry education, plus foundation courses such as English, mathematics, and the humanities. (You're not off the hook just because you're in a vocational or technical program; these skills are important here too.)

Because vocational and technical programs prepare students for entry into industry, community colleges work closely with local industries to make sure that students learn the skills that are actually needed on the job.

Students also receive hands-on experience that reflects the types of workplaces where they will have jobs. Who wants to hire an automotive technician who hasn't worked on a car, or a computer technician who hasn't worked on the latest type of equipment?

FAST FACT: According to the Department of Labor, of the 30 fastest-growing occupations through 2014 (that is, the ones with the largest percent of change in the number of available jobs), 8 of them will require an associate's degree as the level of education needed to enter that occupation. These 8 occupations are: physical therapist assistant, dental hygienist, forensic science technologist, veterinary technologist and technician, diagnostic medical sonographer, occupational therapist, cardiovascular technologist and technician, and paralegal and legal assistant.[3]

Cooperative education experiences (a combined program of paid work and study) or internships (practical work experience related to your field of study; often unpaid) are required by many vocational and technical programs to give students on-the-job training while in college. See Chapter 9 for more information about these programs.

Most degree programs in vocational and technical programs are designed mainly to allow you to enter the job market immediately, rather than to prepare you to transfer to a four-year institution.

Associate in Applied Science (AAS) or Arts (AAA)

When you complete a technical or vocational program of study, you earn an Associate of Applied Science (AAS) degree. This program allows you to develop marketable occupational skills in a particular field of study.

For example, you could earn an AAS degree in food or hotel administration, medical laboratory technology, respiratory therapy, or nursing, and begin work in these fields immediately. With a degree as an aviation maintenance technician and federal licensing, you could start working as a mechanic for a major airline or an air delivery company. You could earn an AAS degree in accounting and get a job as a junior accountant, accounting trainee, or bookkeeper. Or, if you are interested in building trades, you could get an AAS in building trades technology and become a carpenter, plumber, electrician, HVAC technician, or builder, depending on your area of interest. An AAS degree in interior design prepares you for entry-level jobs in this field.

Some institutions now also offer an Associate of Applied or Fine Arts (AAA/AFA) degree focused on preparing students for work in fields such as the fine arts, photography, theater, and music.

Note: The AAS/AAA degree is often considered to be a terminal degree because it is designed for immediate entry into a career rather than as preparation for additional study at an upper division or four-year college. Many credits that you earn for this type of degree may not transfer readily to a bachelor's degree at a four-year institution. If you decide to transfer, you may need to take some additional credits and meet other academic requirements.

Some vocational and technical programs, such as nursing, radiologic technology, and business administration, however, may allow you to transfer easily to a four-year institution for a bachelor's degree. You'll want to check with the college, transfer center, and an academic advisor if you decide you want to go on (see Chapter 10 for more information about the transfer process).

The term *terminal* doesn't mean your educational career has to be at an end! It just means that, at this point, you may be ready to go to work rather than continue your studies for a higher degree.

Certificate

Certificates are awarded for completion of *credit-bearing* coursework related to a specific technical or vocational skill. Certificate programs are meant to give you detailed knowledge in a specialized work area or industry and are designed to help you enter the workforce immediately upon completion. You might, for example, earn a certificate in computer-assisted drafting, interior design and home furnishings, or paralegal studies. If you already have a degree, they can be a great way to enhance your opportunity for a job promotion or enhance your knowledge base in your field.

Certificate programs usually require fewer credits than an associate's degree (often 30 credit hours or less) and typically take about a year or less to complete, if you attend full-time. Sometimes, a certificate can be an intermediate step to earning a degree. At many community colleges, students can receive a certificate after a year or less of study as an intermediate credential and then continue their coursework in the same field for an associate's degree.

PATH 4. LEARNING FOR LIFE AND WORK

The route to a degree is not always direct. Many adults get "hooked" on community college by taking a course for personal enrichment, fun, or for career enhancement or change in continuing education and workforce development programs. These programs are a great way to become familiar with the community college and to test the waters if you think you may be interested in pursuing a more formal course of study leading to a certificate or degree.

Continuing education and workforce development courses are usually affordable, short-term, non-credit courses with convenient schedules and are geared toward the needs of the community and employers. Classes may be held on-campus, at your worksite if your employer has contracted with the college for specialized training, or you may even have the option to take a course online.

These types of courses cover a wide variety of topics and interests aimed at improving your personal knowledge and sharpening work skills. As noted above, adult basic education, English as a Second Language, and high school equivalency are some of the largest programs. Many courses are designed to introduce you to new skills for an entry-level job in a field that interests you (such as health care), enhance your knowledge in a field in which you may already work (such as computer technology), or to prepare you for obtaining a professional license or certification in a field (such as real estate or insurance). Continuing education and workforce development programs can also help you meet professional development and state licensing requirements in fields such as nursing and education. You may need some prior education or work experience depending on what subject you intend to study, but many courses are simply open to anyone who is interested.

You'll be amazed at the variety and range of coursework offered when you check your local community college's schedule of classes for continuing education and workforce programs. Remember educational opportunities for all age ranges—children to senior citizens—which are part of college's efforts to promote life-long learning, are often included in these offerings.

Additional Food for Thought

As you begin to think about what you want to study, consider some of the projections from the U.S. Department of Labor for the years 2004 until 2014.[4]

Computer and healthcare occupations are expected to grow the fastest—that is, they will have the largest percentage of change in the number of available jobs; they will also add 1.8 million jobs during this time. When you look at the educational and training requirements for the occupations that will adding the most new jobs, here's what is expected:

Postsecondary Vocational Award

✓ Nursing aides, orderlies, and attendants

✓ Pre-school teachers, except special education

✓ Automotive service technicians and mechanics

✓ Licensed practical and licensed vocational nurses

✓ Hairdressers, hairstylists, and cosmetologists

Associate's Degree

✓ Registered nurses

✓ Computer support specialists

✓ Dental hygienists

✓ Paralegals and legal assistants

✓ Medical records and health information technicians

If you're looking a little farther into your own future and are thinking of going on to a four-year college, these occupations will be adding the most jobs that require a:

Bachelor's degree

✓ Elementary school teachers (except special education)

✓ Accountants and auditors

✓ Computer software engineers/applications

✓ Computer systems analysts

✓ Secondary school teachers (except special and vocational education)

What Can I Earn?

No matter what path you've chosen in community college, your education will increase your earning ability now and throughout your lifetime. Here are recent U.S. Census Bureau figures on median earnings (median is the midway point in the salary range) for various levels of education:

Median Earnings[5]	
Less than high school graduate	$18,144
High school graduate (includes equivalency degree)	$25,360
Some college or associate's degree	$30,891
Bachelor's degree	$42,404
Graduate or professional degree	$55,065

Whatever way you to choose to start your educational career at community college, you'll be well prepared to find the job of your choice or to continue your studies. The next chapter will tell you what you'll need to consider as you decide whether community college is right for you.

FIND OUT MORE

✦ The best source of information about the full range of programs and training available to you will be found at your community college's Web site and through its publications, such as the college catalog and the schedule of classes.

✦ The U.S. Department of Labor's Web site (www.bls.gov) and especially its *Occupational Handbook* (www.bls.gov/oco/home) are great resources of information about the "hot" areas of employment and educational or training requirements.

✦ www.careervoyages.gov is a federal government Web site that provides up-to-date information about careers, occupations that are in demand, and growth industries for students, parents, and individuals who are changing careers, as well as for career advisors. You'll find information about certificate and two-year degree programs and other alternatives to four-year courses of study.

4

Know Before You Go: How Do I Find Out About Community College?

> *❝ The most important thing anyone can do is to come to the college and talk to someone. It's a big step for someone to walk onto the campus sometimes, but if they do walk through the door, they'll find out about something that will be helpful to them and their future. ❞*
>
> —William H. Zuelke, Department Chair, Advising and Counseling, and Faculty Counselor at Clackamas Community College (Oregon)

Choosing a college is a big decision, and many options are available to you—community college, a four-year institution, or career and technical schools—among others. Attending any college is an investment of time, energy, and money in your future. You'll want to be sure you invest wisely and to make a decision that best suits your personal needs and goals.

Community colleges are as varied as the people and communities they serve. There may be only one community college in your area, or you may have a choice of several different community colleges. They vary in size, programs, services, campus environment, and educational focus, with some placing more emphasis on vocational and technical training and others on preparation for transfer. If a community college is large, there may be multiple branch campuses or centers offering special areas of study such as allied health professions or information technology. You'll want to be sure that the college or campus you choose is right for you by finding out as much as you can about its programs, services, students, and campus before you apply.

You'll never know what a good fit community college could be for you unless you do some research to check it out. This chapter will help you understand the right questions to ask about a community college, understand important factors to consider in your evaluation of a community college, and discover ways to get the information you need to make an informed decision, while having some fun doing it.

What Should I Consider?

Here are some factors you should consider when you're assessing a community college to determine whether or not it's the right one for you.

ACCREDITATION

Make sure that your community college is accredited so that the credits you earn and your degree have value. Accreditation means that a college or its programs meets or exceeds certain basic academic and financial standards set by private nonprofit organizations recognized as accrediting agencies by either the U.S. Department of Education or the Council of Higher Education Accreditation (CHEA).

In addition to accreditation at the institutional level, specialized programs such as nursing or veterinary technical training programs are also evaluated and accredited by professional or industry associations to make sure that their curricula adequately prepare students for their intended occupations.

Why should you care about accreditation? The Council of Higher Education Accreditation cites the following four main reasons (see "Informing the Public about Accreditation" on www.chea.org):

1. Students who want to receive federal (and sometimes state) grants and loans need to be enrolled in an accredited institution or program.

2. A college, university, or program needs to be accredited to be eligible for federal grants and loans or other federal funds.

3. Employers are often concerned about accreditation in several ways—when they provide tuition assistance to employees, when they evaluate your educational credentials for employment, and when they consider making a charitable donation to an institution.

4. State governments require accreditation when making state funds available to students or institutions and when they allow students to take state licensure examinations in some professional fields.

There is also a fifth reason you should care about accreditation:

5. Most four-year colleges and universities will accept transfer credits only from community colleges that are accredited by a regional, national, or professional educational association.

> **TIP:** You can find out if your college or program is accredited by a recognized accrediting agency by checking at the U.S. Department of Education's Web site (www.ope.ed.gov/accreditation).

Accreditation is a voluntary process and it sometimes takes several years for a new institution or program to receive accreditation. It's a goal to which legitimate educational institutions and their programs aspire. It is really an extra validation of quality for an institution and obviously necessary if it wants to receive federal funds. Accreditation also protects you against diploma mills that sell degrees to people, who then find out that the degree neither has value for employment nor transferability of credit to another institution.

If an institution or program is not yet accredited, it may be because it is new, has not yet met minimum standards to be eligible for accreditation, or is in the process of achieving it. Unaccredited institutions are not necessarily of poor quality; it means they have not been evaluated against a set of standards to determine the quality of their education and training.

For the reasons stated above, you can't go wrong, however, by attending an accredited college. Accreditation gives you assurance that the institution and its programs have met a certain standard of quality.

> **FAST FACT:** Employers, educational institutions, and licensing boards—basically your future—are often interested only in degrees from legitimately accredited institutions.

RANGE OF PROGRAMS OFFERED

Community colleges certainly offer a wide range of study options; but no one school can offer everything. It may sound like a no-brainer, but make sure the college offers the program or major that interests you. If you have your heart set on becoming an emergency medical technician, but the community college doesn't offer this course of study, you might need to consider another community college or educational option.

Make sure that the certificate or degree that you want to attain is also offered. The college catalog, available online and in print, is your best guide to this information.

CONVENIENCE OF CLASSES: LOCATION AND CLASS TIME

Community colleges are creative and offer courses in a variety of settings and sometimes at different branch campuses or centers (see Chapter 7 for more on the variety of class locations that may be offered). Be sure to check out the location of programs or courses that interest you. You don't want to find out at the last minute that your classes will be held at a location with which you're unfamiliar or that adds too much time to your commute.

Community colleges also have flexible schedules, but that doesn't mean that every class is given at a time that is convenient for you. Consult the college's schedule of classes for the times and locations of classes that you'll want to take. The schedule is available at the college Web site and also in print from the college's admissions office prior to the beginning of each term.

TIP: At multiple-campus community colleges, the campus where you apply for admission is often your "campus of record." That means your official documents, such as your transcript and official correspondence, are kept at this location. Once admitted, you can take courses on any campus. Keep in mind that some majors and some courses are only offered at selected campuses. Faculty advising and graduation certification may also need to occur at your "campus of record."

Courses or majors may have a distance learning option (see Chapter 7 for more on distance learning), but be sure you know what type of equipment you'll need to access these courses, or where you may need to go to use that equipment. Remember, distance learning comes in all forms—video, CDs, Internet, television courses—so you may still need to be on campus to access some forms of distance instruction, or to attend an orientation or some classes. Don't assume that taking a distance learning course means that you'll never have to be on campus.

FINANCIAL AID

Obtaining financial aid can be a mind-boggling exercise for students of any age, or a student's parents. Having an excellent guide through this process is important. The process of obtaining financial aid can be made easier with solid advisement early on in the application process from the college's financial aid office. In addition, you might be able to apply for financial aid online and get help through the college's Web site. Take a look there first for a preview of how easy or difficult it might be to get a grip on this important aspect of your community college experience. (Chapter 6 covers this subject in greater depth.)

TECHNICAL TRAINING FACILITIES

You won't want to learn about computer hardware and software, printing, or automotive mechanics on out-dated equipment. Because of their strong ties with business and industry, many community colleges have state-of-the-art technology. Take a tour of these facilities yourself to be sure you are satisfied that you'll be learning or practicing on current or relevant equipment.

> **TIP:** Some states require institutions of higher education to provide students, prior to enrollment in a vocational or technical career program, with information about graduation rate, licensing or certificate examination pass rate, and job placement rate. It's good information to have about any program you're considering. Check what data are available from your community college through the admissions office or the specific program that interests you.

STUDENT SUPPORT SERVICES

Community colleges are known for the wide variety of support services available to students. Sometimes, these services are grouped together under a single office, such as "Student Development" or "Student Affairs"; other times, there is a separate office for each type of support service. At a minimum, in addition to the financial aid office, your community college should offer:

1. Academic advisement and counseling services
2. An academic support center or learning resources center to help you succeed in your classes
3. A career center that can help you choose a major related to a career that interests you, prepare you for the world of work, and that can also help you find a job
4. Library facilities with up-to-date technology
5. Access to computers on campus

Many colleges also have services that are geared to special populations, such as returning adults, displaced homemakers, foreign-born students, students in need of English-as-a-Second-Language classes, senior citizens, students with disabilities, and veterans. Check out special services offices that may apply to you.

Make sure you understand what services are available at the campus where you'll spend the most amount of time. Branch campuses and centers often have limited services, and you may find that you need to go to the main campus for some centralized services such as financial aid, career planning, or library facilities.

STUDENT LIFE

What's the campus environment like? Is there somewhere on campus for students to congregate, such as a student activity or multicultural center? What's the cafeteria like and where is it? Even if you're in and out of campus just to take classes, you'll want to know that there's somewhere to get a cup of coffee and sit and study or meet other students.

Is there a range of extracurricular activities and sports in case you have the time or desire to get involved on campus? Participation in extracurricular activities can be a resumé builder. Most campuses have student government, student clubs, and other opportunities to get engaged with the campus. (For more information on the types of extracurricular activities community colleges frequently offer, see Chapter 9.)

FAST FACT: Over 500 two-year institutions belong to the National Junior College Athletic Association, founded in 1938. They may participate in 15 men's and 13 women's sports. If you're not ready for prime-time sports or your college doesn't participate in intercollegiate sports, look for a spot on your community college's intramural teams. See www.njcaa.org for more information.

TRANSFER OPTIONS WITH FOUR-YEAR COLLEGES

Check into what assistance the community college can give you with transferring to a four-year institution, both in- and out-of-state. This can be an easy or complex process, depending on the state in which you live and what types of articulation agreements exist between your community college and four-year institutions. Articulation agreements are agreements that allow for a transfer of course credit between colleges. In other words, credits you earn at community college can count toward your degree at a four-year institution. These agreements are institution-specific, but can be valuable to students who take advantage of them.

You'll need guidance from your community college AND the four-year institution early in your community college career if you intend to transfer. There should be someone on staff who understands the process, can give you guidance, and can troubleshoot for you. See Chapter 10 for an in-depth discussion of the ins and outs of transferring.

REPUTATION

Community colleges are not ranked nationally by publications such as *The Princeton Review* or *U.S. News & World Report,* so you won't be able to find out how your community college rates compared to other ones. Your community college, however, does have a reputation.

It's worth knowing how students rate the college and its services, how they evaluate the faculty, and how both students and community members perceive the college for quality of education and customer service. This information is often available online through surveys conducted by the college. Four-year institutions and employers also know the reputation of your college and will be aware of the quality of instruction you will have received.

TIP: Read your local newspaper to see what's happening at the community college. News about financial problems, faculty or staff disputes, and so on, should raise concerns that you might want to investigate further. Be sure that your community college is financially stable, has a good reputation in the community, and has visible, credible leadership.

Reality Check: A Checklist of Questions You Should Ask

Here is a recap of some of the questions you should ask while researching community colleges to factor into your decision-making process. Only you can determine which factors are most important to you.

❏ Is the college accredited by a recognized accrediting agency? If not, why not?

❏ Does the college have the major or training program that you want?

❏ Is there a flexible schedule of classes in the day, evening, and weekend that works with your schedule?

❏ Are the services you need for admissions, financial aid, career planning, and so on, readily available?

❏ Do you get the feeling you'll be your own, or that you're in a welcoming environment where help is available if you need it and ask for it?

❏ Do you feel comfortable on campus at the times that you'll be taking classes? Is it clear where and when your classes will be held (if there's more than one campus or additional branches or centers) and are they conveniently located for you?

❏ Are there campus facilities that will make studying and being on campus a positive experience?

❏ Is the campus easily accessible, within a reasonable driving distance or commute by public transportation?

❏ Are extracurricular activities such as sports, student organizations, honor societies, and so on, available if you want to be involved?

Reality Check for Nontraditional-Age Students

Adults (nontraditional-age students) who are returning to school often have special concerns and additional questions they need to ask, such as the following:

❏ Is a flexible schedule available? Does the college have a weekend college program or accelerated programs for returning adults?

❏ Are the courses you need available when you can take them? If not, can you take some of them online or through some other available distance learning method?

❏ Can academic credit be given for life or work experience? (See chapter 5 for more information.)

❏ Can you gain credit through exams such as CLEP (College-Level Examination Program)? (See Chapter 5 for more information.)

❏ Are there child-care facilities on campus? Is there a waiting list to enroll a child? Who are the caregivers or teachers? What activities are there? What are the hours?

❏ Are there special services such as orientation, tutoring, or advising, or a special service office for returning adults?

❏ Is there a re-entry program or workshops designed to help returning adults get back in touch with study and test-taking skills?

NOTE TO STUDENTS WITH CHILDREN: While community colleges welcome children with open arms in special programs and day care centers, they aren't usually allowed to be with parents in the classroom, laboratories, libraries, or other places of study on campus. The need to make child-care arrangements—on or off campus—is an ever-present challenge for students with kids.

How Can I Find the Information I Need?

There are many ways to find out about community college, ranging from enrolling in college classes while you're in high school, to personal visits and tours, to discussions with students, faculty, and staff, to the college Web site. You just need to take some time and effort to do a little digging and get a clear picture of what a community college has to offer.

"I advise all students to check out their community college as much as possible through a campus visit, the Web site, and the catalog. It's important for you to find out what they have to offer and feel like you're going to enjoy being there. If you're not comfortable with the college, you're not going to do well."
—Bobbie Page, student at Community College of San Francisco (California)

VISIT YOUR HIGH SCHOOL COUNSELOR

If you are a high school student, your high school guidance counselor will be a good resource about college options, including community college. You may need to take the lead in this conversation, as some counselors may want to steer you directly to a four-year institution.

Ask your counselor about the following:

✓ The benefits of attending community college

✓ Special programs at community college that may be of interest to you

✓ Special scholarship opportunities for high school students who want to attend local community colleges

✓ The comparative cost of community colleges versus four-year institutions

✓ A referral to the admissions or recruiting office at the community college so you can make arrangements for a visit

✓ A schedule of college fairs, visits by community college recruiters, or special opportunities for high school students to go on campus

✓ Special programs that the community college might offer for high school students, such as college transition programs, early admissions and dual enrollment programs, or Tech Prep

✓ Transfer programs between community college and four-year institutions, especially those in state.

The following sections contain information about high school/ community college collaborative programs that may be of interest to high school students and parents. Be sure to ask about these possibilities while you are in the gathering-information process.

GET A HEAD START WHILE YOU'RE IN HIGH SCHOOL

Many high schools and community colleges have collaborative programs for high school students ranging from those for at-risk students who need to strengthen academic and study skills to accelerated programs that allow motivated and academically talents students to take college-level courses while in high school. You or your parents should ask your high school counselors and teachers if your high school participates in or has similar programs your freshman year in high school. You can also check with your local community college to see what opportunities it offers high school students.

Transition Programs for Students

Community colleges often have programs to help make students' transition from high school to college easier. Some are specifically focused on boosting your academic and study skills and to prepare you for college-level courses. Others encourage students to enter college by bringing the college to the high school.

FAST FACT: The Bridge Partnership is an example of a national-level program of selected high schools and community colleges that work together to increase the number of students, especially minorities, who aspire to college by ensuring that students are academically prepared to take college-level courses. See if your high school or local community college participates in this partnership, which is a project of the League for Innovation in Community College. Information can be found at www.league.org/league/projects/bridge.

Austin Community College (Texas), for example, has created "College Connection" with five local school districts to reach out to high school seniors and increase college enrollment, especially among low-income and minority students. At local high schools, community college staff members give students individual help with the college admissions and financial aid process, assessment, orientation and advising, and career planning. Students have a chance to tour Austin Community College's six campuses and to attend "College Day" to learn about academic and workforce programs and degrees. Parents also are involved in information sessions. Students who complete the admissions process receive a letter of acceptance from the college at the same time they receive their high school diploma at graduation.[1]

> **TIP:** Find out from your high school counselor or your local community college (or another college in the area) about federally-funded programs, such as Upward Bound or Talent Search. These programs offer instruction, tutoring, and counseling, plus other activities and services, to help students with academic potential to succeed in their post-high school education. Selected students must meet certain income criteria, be potential first-generation college students, or come from disadvantaged backgrounds (criteria depend on the specific program).

Accelerated Programs

You can be a high school student and a college student at the same time! Check out if your high school has a dual enrollment or early admissions program with your local community college. If you're doing well academically in high school, why not take college-level courses while you finish your high school degree? Granted, this type of program is best for a student who is academically confident, but plenty of you are, so be sure to look into this possibility.

You can take an English, biology, or history course, or a course that isn't offered at your high school. If you want to learn a career skill, such as automotive technology, culinary arts, or information technology, you can take these college-level courses also. Some credits may transfer to a four-year institution.

EARLY ADMISSIONS

High-achieving high school students can apply to community college for early admission and spend their senior year at a community college campus. You will be enrolled in full-time college, taking a full-college courseload (usually 12 credits) each semester, and receiving high school and college credit for courses. Usually, you must also maintain a certain grade-point average to receive your high school diploma.

To participate, you may need to have a specific grade point average, certain scores on your SAT (Scholastic Achievement Test) or ACT, test well on the college's assessment or placement tests, and have a written recommendation from your high school. Criteria vary by high school and college. Your high school counselor should know the details if this option is available at your local community college.

Dual Enrollment

Dual enrollment programs offer high school seniors the opportunity to earn college credit while still attending classes at their regular high school site. It's similar to early admissions, but you're not a full-time college student.

> **SNAPSHOT:** The Community College of Philadelphia offers two types of accelerated programs for high school students. Advance@College gives academically well-prepared students the opportunity to enroll in college-level courses in 11th and 12th grade and earn credits for high school and college. The Advanced Tech at College program allows 30 local high school students to make a seamless transition from high school to an associate's degree program in Computer Information Systems. Students take classes at the college, earn their high school diploma and 24 college credits, participate in an internship in their senior year, tutoring, counseling, and peer study groups. At the end of the program, they earn their high school diploma and 24 college credits.

Advantages of dual enrollment are:

✓ You get a preview of college while in high school.

✓ You might be able to take subjects that aren't offered at your high school.

✓ Some high schools and community colleges allow students to receive credit for high school and college courses at the same time.

✓ You might be able to reduce the time it takes to earn a college degree, which translates into saving money.

Check with your high school or local community college about dual enrollment requirements, which often include getting written permission from your high school principal and your parent or guardian. Many programs also mandate a minimum GPA (grade point average)—find out early so you can earn the grades necessary to participate.

Tech Prep

Getting a head start isn't just for students who want to transfer to a four-year institution. Vocationally and technically oriented students can get a head start with programs such as Tech Prep, a federally funded program that makes the link between high school, community college, and the workforce. It focuses on a planned sequence of study in a technical field, starting as early as the 9th grade. Check with your high school or local community college about Tech Prep program requirements.

This school-to-work transition focuses on two years of occupational study or an apprenticeship program beyond high school. Students who complete the sequence receive a certificate or associate's degree, depending on their field of study. Choices include areas such as engineering technology; applied science; a mechanical, industrial, or practical art or trade; agriculture; health; or business. Tech Prep programs also offer job placement and transfer to applicable four-year baccalaureate programs, as well as career and personal counseling, and occupational assessment.

This type of program can smooth your entry not only into community college and beyond, but also into the workforce.

GET A HEAD START ON ORIENTATION

Some community colleges have preview sessions for high school seniors who intend to enroll at the college the following fall. Montgomery College (Maryland), for instance, offers "How to Succeed in College: The Ultimate New Student Pre-College Experience" in six sessions during the summer. You can get a jump-start on planning your academic program, get a sampler of classes and on-campus activities, and sort out the mysteries of financial aid, as well as brush up on and learn new study skills and how to manage your time.

Adult students should check out the community college's office of adult services to see if there's a special orientation program for returning adults.

> **TIP:** A great way for returning adults to check out a community college is to take a course of interest in continuing education, or through a training course offered by your employer at a community college. Many community colleges also offer college preparation or college skills courses especially geared for adults.

To Whom Should I Talk?

There are various people to whom you should talk in order to find out more about community college. Good sources of information include the college's recruiter, professors, and students—as well as people in the admissions and financial aid offices.

Talk to a Community College Recruiter

You might not think that community colleges make an effort to recruit students, but they don't take it for granted that you'll necessarily turn up on their doorstep just because they're in the neighborhood.

Lea Ann Knight, Director of Counseling and Recruitment at Copiah-Lincoln Community College (Mississippi), outlines her college's strategies: "Our goal is to be the school of choice for high school seniors. We want to try to get the best students from the best high schools in the areas to consider Copiah-Lincoln as a first step and then transfer to a four-year school when they graduate. We also recruit heavily for our Career-Technical program, which prepares students for the workforce after one or two years of training in one of the 21 different programs we offer. Four-year colleges aren't our only competition. There are two community colleges within 40 miles of us, which are within driving distance for many of the students who are eligible to attend them for no additional fee."

Her office conducts regular outreach activities to the 21 high schools in the seven counties served. In the fall, staff members participate in high school college fairs (see "Go to the College Fair" later in this section) and conduct college prep workshops in each senior English classroom.

"In the spring, we go one step further and invite students from all 21 high schools in the area to come to campus for our high school days. We also follow up with seniors who have indicated they might or will attend the college. In addition, we identify students with strong academic records who might qualify for scholarship funds. Our staff is special in that everyone has attended Copiah-Lincoln Community College. It's easy to sell something you believe in," says Mrs. Knight.

> **SNAPSHOT:** You never know when some information you learned about community college will be useful. Keith Armstrong, a detective in Jersey City, New Jersey, and a student at Hudson County Community College (New Jersey) heard a talk by the head of the college's criminal justice program several years before he decided to enroll. The college representative had come to the police department to encourage police officers to continue their education. Detective Armstrong says, "I remembered that talk when I was thinking about enrolling in community college and it motivated me to finally enroll in that program."

Talk to a Professor

Make an appointment to speak with a professor in your proposed area of study, if you know it. Get a sense of what courses are needed for your field, special entry requirements, class size, honors classes or other special opportunities, career opportunities and job prospects, departmental scholarships, and so on. You'll be able to put a name with a face even if you don't take a class with that instructor.

Don't be shy about asking some questions like the following:

✓ How do successful students balance their studies, work, and family life?

✓ What do community college instructors expect of their students?

✓ What happens if I get in trouble academically or have personal problems?

✓ What resources are available to help me be successful?

✓ What types of jobs do people in my area of interest get?

Talk to a Current Community College Student or a Graduate

Someone you know may be attending a community college. Ask around. The best sources about what your school will be like are someone who went there recently, or, even better, someone who is a current student. You can find plenty of people in the community, or perhaps even your own friends or a family member, who can give you a firsthand account of what to expect. Your experience won't be exactly the same, but you can learn from their experiences!

Returning adults, for example, might be anxious about being in classes with younger students (and vice versa). Hearing about another adult's interaction with other students and professors, how they juggled work, family, and school, can be a big help in alleviating any fears about enrolling or being able to succeed.

If you can't find a current student or alumnus (a graduate of the college), contact the college's alumni office or office of communications. They'll be glad to put you in touch with an alumnus or a current student.

> **TIP:** Attending a sports event, a workshop through a continuing education program, or a cultural event on campus are great ways to get a feel for the campus environment. Many community colleges also have programs for the entire family including special summer programs for school-age children and teens.

GO TO THE COLLEGE FAIR

Community colleges send their recruiters to college fairs, so be sure to look for their booths. A college fair brings together representatives of many colleges so that you can meet them and gather information about several colleges in one convenient place. They're usually held in the fall and spring.

Your high school might host a college fair with other high schools; a local business, civic association, or a college in the area might also host a fair. Students of all ages are welcome to attend, so adults thinking about going back to school should also take advantage of fairs.

You might be tempted to pass by your local community college's booth, thinking that you can always get information about the local school. Instead, plan to make a stop and allow yourself some time to hear what their representatives have to say.

You'll find out more in person than you expected, plus you'll have a contact if you have questions, decide to follow-up with an application, or once you get on campus. Don't underestimate the power of personal contact. In addition, you may be able to speak with a student from the school who is on site to help with recruitment.

TIP: Check with your high school counselor, look online at various college Web sites for college fair postings, and check your local newspaper. The National Association of College Admissions Counselors (www.www.nacacnet.org) sponsors the National College Fair program and has a complete schedule of fairs in major cities on its Web site, plus tips for parents and students interested in going to a fair.

Have a few prepared questions, especially if you have a choice of several community colleges in your area:

✓ What makes this community college special and why should I consider enrolling?

✓ Are there any special programs or services that I should know about that will make my transition to college easier?

✓ Are there special programs, such as honors classes, cooperative education experiences, internships, or study-abroad opportunities, that might make this experience more rewarding than I anticipate?

✓ What percentages of students are enrolled in transfer programs versus vocational/technical programs?

✓ How would you describe the campus environment?

✓ Tell me about the types of students who go to college here.

✓ How much will it cost to attend? What will my savings be over an in- or out-of-state four-year institution?

Can't make the fair? Recruiters also make presentations at high schools, local organizations, churches, and other community locations, so just because you missed the fall or spring college fair doesn't mean you've missed the opportunity to hear about the college.

SEE THE COLLEGE CAMPUS WITH YOUR OWN EYES

Seeing and hearing about a community college in person is the best way to decide whether or not it's right for you.

SNAPSHOT: Travis Huelsebusch says: "I heard about the Aviation Maintenance Technology program at Cincinnati State Technical and Community College when instructors came to my high school 'Aerospace Academy' classes that were held at the local airport. I was impressed by them and the video I saw about the college's aeronautics facility in Harrison, Ohio. The college reps invited us to tour the facility. We got to sit in on a class, meet some of the faculty, and see the labs. It was very impressive, and I decided that this was the place for me to start."

Try to visit the campus during the time you think you'll be attending classes. If you'll be a day student, visit during the week while classes are in session. If you'll be an evening student, make a visit at night to see if you feel safe and comfortable getting to the campus and on campus, especially if you are a woman. Get a feel for the degree of on-campus activity, and see what offices and services will still be open and available for evening students.

Many colleges have student ambassadors or guides who volunteer to show parents and prospective students around the campus. You can hear firsthand what it's like to be a student at that particular community college while you tour the facilities.

Todd Sullivan, a recent graduate of Copiah-Lincoln Community College (Mississippi), served as a Trailblazer, a peer recruiter and ambassador for the college. He says, "You have to apply for a position and be selected. Trailblazers serve as host and hostesses at campus events, especially for visits by parents and students. We also manned the booths and tables at college fairs so that prospective students had a current student's perspective on the college. You can find out a lot from another student that you might not learn from someone else. Students also like to speak with other students because there may be questions they don't feel comfortable asking college staff."

Also, talk to other students you encounter on campus to get the non-official version of what's what on campus. From such impromptu discussions, you'll get a good idea of the college's pros and cons.

Here are some questions to ask:

- ✓ What are the best features about the college? What is a feature of the college that you, as a guide, don't usually draw attention to?
- ✓ What's something that I should know that isn't in the brochure or online?
- ✓ How large will my classes be?
- ✓ How accessible will my professors be?
- ✓ What's it like to be a student on this campus?
- ✓ What does the college do to help students who aren't sure what program of study or career they are interested in?

✓ What are some features of the college that surprised you when you first came here?

✓ What are some things you would have liked to have known before you enrolled here, but didn't find out until later?

TIP FOR PARENTS: A visit to the college might be your best chance to ease any concerns you have about your son or daughter attending community college, their ability to transfer credits to another institution, and to ask questions about financial aid. Let your student take the lead in the conversations and fill in with any questions you have.

Reality Check: Things to Do During a Campus Visit

When you visit the community college campus, consider doing some of the following activities:

❑ Stop by the admissions office, pick up a college catalog, schedule of classes, and application materials. Talk to someone about your possible interest in enrolling and any concerns you have.

❑ Check out how you'll be received in a department by simply going in and asking some questions. Tell them you're thinking of enrolling.

❑ Set up an appointment with a professor or department head before your visit by phone or email. Remember, people love to talk about what they do and are glad to share information about the college. Don't be afraid to ask about things that concern you.

❑ Talk with representatives of school clubs about extracurricular activities.

❑ With permission, sit in on a class or several classes.

❑ Visit the athletic and health/wellness facilities.

❏ Sample the food in the cafeteria. Creature comforts are important.

❏ Visit the career center to see how they can help you focus on a major if you're undecided about what to do, and check on work opportunities on campus.

❏ Pick up information from the financial aid office about scholarship opportunities directly from the college.

❏ If you are a disabled student, returning adult student, senior citizen, displaced homemaker, veteran, woman, or international student, see if there are special offices or programs for services for you.

❏ Check on accessibility of computer labs and facilities, especially if you don't have a computer at home.

❏ Visit the library facilities and learning resource center to see what type of help is available.

❏ Tour the relevant facility for the vocational/technical programs that interest you to check out their equipment or labs.

❏ If there are dorms available, get a preview of your living space. You don't want to be surprised when you pull up to unload your belongings and find there isn't enough space for that television you just bought.

❏ Check out parking on campus.

❏ Grab a copy of the college newspaper and read the bulletin boards. They'll give you a sense of campus life.

TIP: Students with disabilities should check out how accessible the campus is. Is it wheelchair friendly? Is there escort assistance for students who need help? Are classrooms equipped for students with special needs? Is assistive technology available? A visit to the office that serves students with disabilities can be of invaluable assistance in determining if a community college is the right place for you.

Take the Campus' Pulse at Open Houses and Other On-Campus Events

If you don't have time for an extensive campus tour, there's a shorter version. Many community colleges run a series of open houses in the fall and spring so you can get a sense of the campus environment, available programs, services, and extracurricular activities. Just walking around can give you a feel for whether nor not you feel comfortable in that college's environment. You can chat with students, professors, and staff to make sure that the programs you want to pursue are offered and to get the pulse of campus life.

Make an Electronic and Virtual Visit

Don't have the time to visit the campus in person? The community college Web site is a gold mine of information about all aspects of the college, ranging from its history, campus facilities, and academic programs to student services and more. It's worth a quick look online to be sure that the community college has the major or program you're interested in pursuing. Even if you can visit the campus, the college Web site is a great place to get an overview or as much detail as you want about a college. If you don't have access at home to a computer, your local library may have availability. Your college's Web site may post information about such things as:

✓ The college's history, mission, and accreditation and the student population

✓ Academic and campus event calendar

✓ Campus directory so you can email or call for information

✓ Campus map and directions

✓ Admissions process and application information

✓ Assessment and placement testing

✓ The college catalog with majors and requirements

✓ Financial aid process and applications

✓ Orientation sessions

✓ Information about campus services and facilities

✓ Faculty members' Web pages with their credentials, areas of expertise, courses they instruct, and their contact information

✓ Student evaluations of services and faculty

✓ Student organizations

✓ College publications, including the newspaper (Read it! You can get the inside story about what's going on.)

✓ Housing, if any; cultural, athletic, and health/wellness and other facilities

You may even be able to take a virtual tour of the campus online and get a sense of what the facilities are like without having to make a visit in person.

> **TIP:** Look online at the college's office of institutional research for a quick overview of the college's student enrollment, faculty, graduation statistics, and other data about the institution.

Final Deciding Factors

If you have followed all the suggestions above, you now have full and complete information about your community college of interest. Here are a few final suggestions.

DRIVE IT

Drive to the community college and see how long it takes you. Or, try to reach it by public transportation and see if the commute is reasonable. You'd be surprised how many students find transportation becomes an unexpected challenge that can interfere with on-time and regular attendance.

By driving there or checking out how long the bus or train takes, you'll be ahead of the game and will be prepared to factor that into your planning. You'll also want to check on the availability (and expense) of parking, or how long (and safe) the walk to campus is from the bus or subway stop or parking lot.

If the drive is too long, see if dorms are available or if the campus can direct you to affordable off-campus housing. Find out also what types of distance learning options are available.

> **TIP:** Take a test drive to the campus where most of your classes will be held about the time they will be held. You'll get a good idea of traffic flow and volume and length of your commute. If you're going by public transportation, test out how long the bus or train trip is. Factor that commuting time into the amount of time you need to devote to going to school.

TRUST YOUR INSTINCTS

Among the many factors to consider when you are selecting a college or deciding to enroll is your gut-level feeling about what's right for you. When you walk onto a campus, you should have a positive feeling that you'll be pleased to spend two years of your time and money there.

Karen Freeman, valedictorian of her high school class and graduate of Copiah-Lincoln Community College, Mississippi, Class of 2005, says, "Having attended summer classes at a four-year college between my junior and senior year in high school, I knew what it was like to be on a big campus and in large classes. I could have had a full-tuition scholarship there, but I decided that Copiah-Lincoln was right for me. It was close to home, my parents and brothers all had good experiences there, and they offered me a great financial package. Copiah-Lincoln also had a reputation for its excellent science programs. All those factors made me realize that community college was the right place for me to be at that time of my life. I'm now enrolled in a pharmacy program at Ole Miss, where I was one of the top five applicants to the program."

Find Out More

+ www.pathwaystocollege.net has an online database of over 1,100 pre-college outreach programs including those at community colleges.

+ Sallie Mae, a corporate provider of federally guaranteed student loans, has a Web site at www.collegeanswer.com that offers excellent information about planning to attend college, including a discussion about various types of colleges, specific information about types of colleges, timelines, checklists, and good common-sense advice. Specific information about community college is offered.

Knock, Knock: How Do I Get In?

5

> *Enrolling in community college is like Christmas shopping. If you shop early, every-thing you want is available and lines are short. At community college, if you wait until August to enroll for the fall semester, you'll find you may not get the schedule of classes you want and lines will be long. Come see us as early as possible and avoid the crowd.*
>
> —Dale Smith, Associate Professor and Counselor, Office of Admissions, Westchester Community College (New York)

It may be easier to be accepted into a community college than a four-year school, but open admission doesn't mean you can just walk on campus and start classes. There's still some paperwork to do before you get in and once you are admitted!

In this chapter, you'll learn about how to apply and be admitted to community college and what resources will be available to you to help you select a program of study. You'll also find out about how to get credit for prior educational or work experience. Students with disabilities and international students will also find information about their special admissions concerns.

71

What Do I Need to Be Admitted?

Community colleges pride themselves on their "open door" or open admissions policies that do not impose many restrictions on admission—that is, the process of being officially recognized as a student at a college. Each community college, however, has its own admissions policies and requirements for documents you must have if you want to be accepted and enroll in courses *for credit*. So, you definitely should check with the college's Admissions Office before making your application.

If you're interested in taking *non-credit courses* through continuing education or workforce development, you can often directly register for and enroll in these courses. You don't usually need to meet the same admissions requirements as students enrolling in for-credit coursework (although you may need to meet certain requirements or have educational or work experience to enroll in a particular course!).

> **REALITY CHECK:** Open admission doesn't mean there are no deadlines! You need to get your paperwork completed and transcripts (your official record of grades) sent at least 6–8 weeks before the start of a semester or quarter.

If you are a first-time student at the college, you will need to complete an application for admission and submit it with an application fee, as well as some of the documents described below, before being admitted to the college.

Many community colleges have *rolling admissions,* that is, you can submit your application for admission at any time during the year. You will, however, need to indicate when you intend to begin your studies. For example, you may apply to be admitted in the fall or spring semester of a particular academic year.

Usually, once you are admitted, you do not have to go through this process again unless you stop attending for an extended period of time.

PAPERS, PAPERS, PAPERS

Generally speaking, if you have an official high school diploma or GED certificate (general education diploma; also called *high school equivalency*), you will be eligible for admission to community college to take coursework for credit. Some colleges also require that you be at least 18 years of age (16 in some states) to be admitted. For your application, you'll need an official transcript (the records of your grades) from your high school as well as verification that you have graduated.

If you have special circumstances—you do not have a diploma or GED, have been home schooled, or are 16 years or younger—it's best to check with the Admissions Office about additional requirements. Remember, you can study for your GED or your high school diploma at community college.

> **TIP:** If you're a high school student, sit down early with your high school counselor and review your coursework and credits to make sure you will fulfill all the requirements of high school for graduation. Take this step early in your junior year so you won't be surprised, find that you're missing a credit or two, and have to delay entry into college.

Although most community colleges do not require them for admittance, some do want SAT (Scholastic Aptitude Test) or ACT (American College Test) scores for recent high school graduates. If you have taken either of these college entrance exams, the results can be helpful for placement purposes or for gaining advanced credit (discussed later in this chapter). Also, these test scores may be required or helpful if you want to enter an honors program or honors courses.

Note: Letters of recommendation, essays, or interviews are rarely part of the community college admissions process.

> **TRANSFER STUDENTS:** If you have attended another community college or four-year institution, you'll want to check with the college to which you are applying about admissions requirements, test requirements, transcripts, and credit for previous coursework.

RESIDENCY REQUIREMENTS

Community colleges often serve specific designated geographic areas and the population that lives in that area. This doesn't mean that they don't accept other students, but they may give preference for admission and special tuition rates to students who are considered to be residents of the area they serve. The state in which you live may also have residency requirements that can impact the tuition rate you will pay at a community college. If you have a question about your residency status, check with the admissions office (see Chapter 6 for more information about financial issues).

NEED SHOTS?

Some educational systems require documented proof of immunization from a physician for one or more communicable diseases, such as measles, chicken pox, tetanus, diphtheria, or hepatitis. The requirements for some immunizations may be age-related; that is, students born after a certain date will need to have proof for a particular disease(s). Other types of immunizations may be required of *all* students.

Find out if you need any immunizations. If you do, get ready to stick out your arm and say "Ouch!"

ADMISSION TO SPECIFIC PROGRAMS

Meeting the general overall admissions requirements to take for-credit courses at a community college gets your foot in the door of the college. *It does not, however, mean that you are admitted to a particular program of study.*

Individual departments and programs may have specific admission requirements that students must first meet before being able to pursue studies in a particular subject area.

Some programs, especially in the health professions, are highly selective and competitive, and have strict admissions requirements. For example, to be admitted to a registered nursing program, you may need a certain grade point average, completion of certain courses in biology, chemistry, anatomy or physiology, and a certain level of proficiency in subjects such as English and mathematics *before* you can apply for admission to the program. Once you do apply and are admitted, your final admission to the nursing program may depend on additional requirements.

Selective programs may also admit students only as part of a group at the beginning of the academic year or semester, and may have space limitations.

Don't be disappointed! Check out the program of study you're considering *beforehand* to see what its requirements are and if you meet the criteria. If you don't, you may have to bring up your grade point average, fulfill some prerequisites (coursework required before you enter a program or take a higher level course), and brush up on basic language, science, or mathematics skills. The department or program in question will be able to tell you what you need to do to meet its requirements.

Here's a reminder about some of the documents you will need to apply to community college and be admitted.

Admission Checklist

Do I have?

- ❑ Application form, available online or at the admissions office of the college
- ❑ Application fee
- ❑ An official high school diploma and transcript, or a GED certificate
- ❑ Admission test scores for the SAT/ACT, if required (also useful to have if you are seeking advanced standing)
- ❑ Proof of residency
- ❑ Proof of immunization, if required
- ❑ Any special documentation required, such as an audition tape or portfolio for a music or art program

ADULT LEARNERS: See if your community college has an office to address your special concerns and for information about admissions, registration, high school equivalency diploma, evaluation of transfer credit, and credit through examination or life experience. There may be a special program to help you brush up on study skills and orient you to the campus. Counseling for personal, academic, and financial concerns may also be available through this office.

Testing, Testing

Once you're admitted to the college, you might be surprised by the next step: You'll need to take some tests to assess your language, writing, reading, and mathematics abilities. So sharpen your pencils and your computer skills. Almost everyone has to take these tests, unless you have an exemption (see below).

TIP: Get a head start on the assessment and placement tests. Some colleges offer sample tests online, or use standardized tests, such as Accuplacer, that also have sample tests available online. You can get an idea of what you'll be facing at the assessment and testing center.

Don't worry. These tests are meant to help you succeed in your college-level courses. If you've been out of school for a while, think about them as "refresher" courses that will help you sharpen your skills in areas where you could be a bit rusty. The tests assess if you need additional preparation in basic skills and can help place you in the appropriate level of coursework in a particular subject area.

Depending on your test results, you may need to take one or more basic skills courses (also called *developmental* courses) in math, writing, reading, or English language skills *before* enrolling in credit-bearing courses.

If you've tested well in one area, such as mathematics, but need assistance in another area such as writing, you could enroll in a college-level math course while taking a basic skills course to strengthen your writing skills. Or you may test well in all areas and be able to proceed directly to college-level courses.

It could take several semesters to complete all your basic skills coursework. This coursework does count toward your status as a part-time or full-time student, that is, the number of hours in which you are enrolled each term. It does not, however, carry any academic credit that will count toward your certificate or degree requirements. Basic skills courses will, however, help you get a good foundation for your future success.

Keith Armstrong, a detective in Jersey City (New Jersey) and a returning adult student at Hudson County Community College (New Jersey), said, "I took the placement tests and did well on the math tests, but found out my writing skills weren't up to par. I had to take some basic-level English classes first, which worked out well. They gave me a very good foundation for the writing I needed to do in my other classes. In fact, one of my English professors liked my essays so much (to my surprise) that he invited me to attend an honors-level writing course. Learning the basics also helped me at work, where I have to write reports nearly every day."

TIP: Your mother was right! You need to know how to type!! Computers have almost replaced pen and pencil for taking skills and assessment tests. So if your computer skills are non-existent or not up to par, take a basic computer course and learn the ropes. Your life will be easier every step of the way—from accessing information about the college online to completing admissions forms, enrolling in courses of your choice, to doing actual coursework.

TESTING OUT

Depending on your college's policy, you may be exempt from taking assessment or placement tests if

✓ You have earned a degree from an accredited U.S. college or university.

✓ You have completed a college-level English or mathematics course at an accredited U.S. college or university.

✓ You have earned certain scores, as specified by the college, on standardized tests such as the SAT, ACT, TOEFL (Test of English as a Foreign Language), or Advanced Placement tests. See "Get Credit for What You Already Know" later in this chapter.

Get Credit for What You Already Know

Once you're admitted to a college, see what options there are for receiving credit for prior knowledge and learning experiences, especially if you're an adult learner. Standards are high, so it's not a breeze to get credit this way, but you could save some time and money.

In addition to taking community college courses while in high school, as discussed in Chapter 4, there are several other ways to turn knowledge and experience gained through formal and informal means—such as on-the-job training, independent study, or life experience—into a head start on your college degree or certificate. Normally, you will need to be admitted to the college before pursuing this type of credit. Common methods include:

✓ Credit earned in high school (such as dual enrollment or Tech Prep, discussed in Chapter 4)

✓ Credit by examination or certification

✓ Credit for nontraditional programs or life experience

✓ Credit by transfer

Some colleges allow you to earn credit; others may not award credit but allow you to bypass or waive certain introductory courses, or advance to another level of coursework. Because college policies and standards differ, be sure to check with the office of admissions or registrar about what options are available to you. Usually, the college catalog will have the policies listed under a heading such as "Advanced Standing" or "Credit-by-Examination."

CREDITS EARNED THROUGH EXAMINATION OR CERTIFICATION

Some common ways that you can earn credit by examination are:

✓ **Advanced Placement (AP) examinations.** If you've recently taken Advancement Placement courses and examinations in high school or through independent study, your prospective community college may award you credits in certain subject areas, depending on your exam scores and their policy.

✓ **College-Level Examination Program (CLEP).** Taking CLEP exams, which test for material covered in introductory college courses, are a common way to earn credit by exam. You may have acquired the knowledge through self-study, your job or life experience, home schooling, advanced courses in high school, or many other ways.

Depending on your community college's policy, you may be able to earn 3 to12 credits per exam taken if you earn a passing score. CLEP exams are given in 34 specific subject areas and 5 liberal arts areas (English Composition, Humanities, Mathematics, Social Science and History, and Natural Science).

Most CLEP exams, except English Composition with Essay, are multiple choice or fill-in-the-blank type questions and take 90 minutes to complete. (Language exams usually have a listening component.) CLEP is *only given by computer* at various college testing sites around the country. There is a charge for each exam taken.

FAST FACT: The College-Level Examination Program (CLEP) is the most widely accepted credit-by-examination program in the United States. There are 2,900 institutions that grant credit for CLEP. Each one sets its own CLEP policy about exams for which credit is awarded, scores required for credit, and how much credit will be given.[1]

✓ **Credit by Departmental Examination.** Your community college may allow you to take a department-based examination in a specific subject such as a foreign language, mathematics, or computer science to demonstrate your understanding of skills and concepts covered by a college-level course. If you pass, you may be able to earn credit for that course or waive prerequisites for higher-level courses. Departmental examinations are often challenging examinations similar to a course's final examination.

✓ **Credit for Certification.** If you have earned certification in a field such as Licensed Practical Nursing, Medical Laboratory Technician, the National Institute for Automotive Service Excellence Automotive Technician Certification Tests, or in another vocational or technical field, your community college may award you credit. Certain restrictions and requirements apply, but it's worth checking out.

TIP: If you are or were in the military, look into DANTES (Defense Activity for Nontraditional Educational Support) as a way to earn college credit by examination for subjects normally taught in introductory college courses. DANTES offers a testing program, evaluation of military technical training, and prior learning portfolio development. DANTES exams are open to nonmilitary individuals also. See www.dantes.doded.mil for additional information.

CREDITS FOR NONTRADITIONAL PROGRAMS AND LIFE EXPERIENCE

You'll be surprised to find how your life and work experience can count for college credit. You'll spend some time to document your experiences, but it may help you get a head start.

✓ **Workplace Training.** Training that you have received in the workplace and through military service courses, computer certification coursework, or through various academies recognized by your community college, such as a police and corrections academy or a federal government training center, may also allow you to qualify for credit, advanced standing, or a waiver of certain requirements.

✓ **Portfolio Evaluation Program.** Your life or work experience may earn you college credit at some community colleges through a portfolio evaluation.

A portfolio is a written record of specific experience, accomplishments, knowledge, and documentation of learning related to the courses for which you would like credit or the degree you want to pursue.

Typical elements of a portfolio include a life history essay; a statement about your short- and long-term goals; a discussion of major accomplishments and supporting documentation such as a performance evaluation from work, transcripts, and samples of work; and a narrative about your learning experience and how it relates to the core learning outcomes of the course(s) for which you are seeking credit.

Faculty members in specific subject areas then evaluate the portfolio for credit.

Creating a portfolio is not easy! Many community colleges will require you to take a Portfolio Development course to help guide you through the process.

✓ **International Baccalaureate.** The Swiss-based International Baccalaureate Organization, a nonprofit educational foundation, offers a curriculum and diploma recognized by colleges and universities worldwide. Check with your prospective community college to see if they offer credit for this exam-based diploma or coursework taken through this program.

CREDIT BY TRANSFER

If you've earned college credit at another educational institution, be sure to speak to a transfer counselor about whether or not your credits will count at your community college. You already paid for them elsewhere, so it's worth seeing if you can get credit at your new institution.

Transfer credit for vocational/technical coursework may be accepted by your college, but it's more the exception than the rule, and may also have time limitations.

Community colleges will also consider credit for military service school courses and skills, so be sure to check on your college's policy if you're a veteran or an active-duty service member.

> **TIP:** An official transcript is required to ensure authenticity. That means one that has the seal of the institution and the signature of an official from that institution. Usually, a transcript is acceptable only if sent directly from the transferring institution to your community college.

If you are a foreign-born student or have taken college-level coursework overseas, you'll need to have your courses evaluated by an outside evaluation firm to see if the credits will transfer to your new college. See the end of the chapter for information on this type of service.

Check Out Financial Aid, ASAP!

In addition to knowing what documents you'll need to complete your application for admission, you'll want to start exploring financial aid options early. Don't tackle this on your own. It's complicated, so let an on-campus expert in the financial aid office help you understand your options and direct you to some sources of aid that you might not know about.

You can speak with a financial aid counselor to discover how you can apply for aid *before* you apply to the college. Financial aid typically requires a long processing time. You won't want to be admitted to the college and then find that you don't have the financial aid money available yet to pay for tuition and fees. See Chapter 6 for more details about financial aid.

How Will I Know What Courses to Take?

Once you've been admitted to the college, there will still be more to do! Being admitted *does not* mean that you are registered. When you select, schedule, and enroll (secure a place) in your classes, you'll be officially registered. The college will able to record and track your academic progress. You need to register and enroll in classes each term. You'll also need some advice about what to take based on your interests, personal schedule, and educational goals. You'll have experts and resources available to you to help you make these decisions.

CHOOSING A PROGRAM OF STUDY

You may be fortunate enough to know exactly what major (your primary field of study) or career you want to pursue. If you don't know, don't panic. Many students enter community college without a clear idea of what they want to study, or what types of jobs they can get when they study a particular subject.

You can, however, begin to explore choices. The earlier you begin, the better chance you have to create a long-term road map for achieving your associate's degree or certificate, or for transferring to a four-year institution. There are plenty of resources and people on campus to help you make a decision. Keep reading for more information.

> **FAST FACT:** Many community colleges offer an Associate's degree in General Studies (AGS) for students who want maximum flexibility in meeting requirements for transfer to a four-year institution, exploring a career, or meeting other personal goals.

WHAT YOU'LL NEED TO TAKE

You'll need to fulfill requirements for your certificate or degree by balancing courses and meeting requirements in several different areas:

1. General education requirements
2. Courses in your major (your primary field of study)
3. Electives (courses that interest you but that may not be related to your major)

If you intend to transfer to a four-year college or university, you'll also want to be sure that you're taking courses for which you'll get credit when you are admitted to that institution. (See Chapter 10 for more information on transferring.)

You'll want to create a checklist of all the requirements you need to meet and keep track of your progress each semester.

General Education Requirements

Many community colleges have *general education require- ments*, also called *general core curriculum* (course of study) *requirements*. These are courses that all students need to fulfill to have a well-rounded education.

The core curriculum is centered on subjects such as English composition, mathematics, arts, humanities, social and behavioral sciences, and natural sciences. Students in vocational and techni- cal programs are also required to take the "core courses." Many of these courses are ones you'll take in your first several semesters at college.

You may think that the core's a bore, or that it will take you off track from your career interests. Try to look at these courses as an opportunity to explore a subject you might enjoy or as a way to help you select a major. They might be your best chance to explore a field that you didn't even know interested you, or to dig into something you always wanted to know about, but simply didn't have time to learn about.

> **FAST FACT:** If you've already graduated with an AA or AS degree (usually in a non-vocational/technical field) or have a higher degree from a regionally accredited U.S. institution of higher education, the community college might consider that you have met some or all general education requirements, depending on your major.

Deciding On a Major

You won't need to declare (choose) a major, the primary subject you have decided to study, the moment you are admitted, but it's good to start thinking about your major sooner rather than later if you want to earn your degree in a specific field.

For example, you may choose to major in English, computer science, or accounting. The majority of courses that you take will be in the field of study you choose. If you are undecided about a major, don't worry. You can follow a course of study in general studies and still get your associate's degree.

It's important to realize that choosing a major isn't always the same as choosing a career. If you study math as your major, it doesn't mean you have to be a mathematician when you graduate. Your major can be the broad base for a number of different career options. Majoring in math, for example, might prepare you for a variety of careers in science, business, insurance, or engineering.

It's also important to understand that once you've chosen a major, it doesn't mean you're stuck with it. You can change your mind if you think you've made a mistake, or find that the selection you've made won't lead you where you want to go.

Most students change their minds at least once about what they want to study. But you don't want to change majors too often, as it can cost you time and money to start over in a new area.

Once you do decide on a major, you'll want to examine the required coursework, be sure you understand what the prerequisites are, and know the number of credits you must earn to complete the degree or certificate in that major. The sooner you choose a major, the more time you'll be able to spend taking courses that count toward your degree.

Academic advisors, professors, and career centers are are all resources that are available to help you choose a major.

SNAPSHOTS: Matt Starr studies automotive technology at the Horace S. Gudelsky Institute for Technical Education at Montgomery College (Maryland). Matt started out taking computer and art courses, which he is still pursuing, but saw an introductory course in automotive mechanics in the college catalog. He decided he wanted to learn how to repair his own car, and enrolled in the course. "I don't know what I'll do in the long run, but I'm working part-time in the automotive program and can get an ASE master technician's certificate if I complete the associate's degree and pass the National Institute for Automotive Service Excellence (ASE) technician certification exams. Everyone needs his car repaired so it's a good safety net even if I decide to pursue art or computers as a career."

His co-worker in the program, Oleg Yurchak, finished his AA degree in automotive technology and has decided to study for an associate's degree in mechanical engineering and then try for a bachelor's degree at a four-year institution. He says, "The automotive program is great training for a mechanical engineering degree because you get hands-on experience with sophisticated machinery. The training here is so good that you're almost guaranteed to pass the ASE exam, which guarantees you a better starting salary. I'll always have the option of finding a job in the automotive field or in engineering."

Elective Courses

In most fields of study, you'll also be able to take some coursework outside your major. Courses that will count toward your degree or certificate, but which are not required for your major, are called *electives*.

These are courses that may complement your major or that you choose just because they interest you. For example, if you're majoring in English, you might choose an elective course in communications as a related field, or in accounting as an unrelated field.

Vocational/technical programs tend to have a more defined curriculum (course of study) and often do not offer as many opportunities for elective coursework as do liberal arts-based programs of study.

TRANSFER CONSIDERATIONS

If you think you'll want to transfer to a four-year institution, you'll want to select courses early on that will transfer smoothly to the institution you want to attend. You may even be in a special transfer studies program geared especially to this goal of helping you switch into a four-year institution and helping you prepare for a major there. Different four-year colleges have different requirements for transfer. See Chapter 10 for more information about transferring.

Getting Help Making Decisions

You'll be in luck at community college because there will be many sources of assistance and advice to help you plan your program of study—right from your first day of classes through to graduation. You'll want to take advantage of all available resources—the college catalog, schedule of classes, academic advisers, the career center—to help you stay on track.

USE YOUR COLLEGE CATALOG

One of your best and most important sources of information about the college is the college catalog, available online and in print from the college. The catalog will be a very important tool in helping you plan your course of study and understanding the requirements you must meet to complete your certificate or degree. It will help you answer questions such as" What are the college's requirements for graduation? What are the courses I need to take in my major in order to graduate?"

The catalog includes general information about the college's mission and philosophy, campus locations and directions, admissions, tuition and fees, financial aid, student services, academic standards, and special programs.

It also outlines all the programs of study (curricula) with all course requirements and in what order you should take these courses. You'll find detailed descriptions about each individual course so you can easily understand what the course is about, the number of credits you will earn for the course, and any pre-requisites (courses you need to take prior to another course), and other important information. Requirements for fulfilling your major and for graduating are also in the catalog.

The college catalog will also identify all the offices on campus, their staff, and the faculty members of the college. The catalog will outline many of the college's policies on issues such as smoking, discrimination, and sexual harassment.

Before or when you register for courses, be sure to get a copy of the catalog relevant to the year you are admitted because it sets out the requirements you must meet to complete your degree or certificate, and to graduate. Even if requirements change over time, you will need to meet the ones in place at the time you were first admitted and enrolled. Keep your catalog and refer to it frequently!

BE ON TIME: KNOW THE SCHEDULE AND DEADLINES

The *schedule of classes* lists all the classes that will be offered during a particular term and includes days, times, and location of classes plus the instructor's name. It is usually available in print and online.

The schedule of classes will be your guide to when enrollment or registration begins for the semester or quarter, when tuition payments are due, when classes begin and end, the last day to drop or add courses, the last day to withdraw from a course without a grade penalty, the examination schedule, and the date for commencement.

TIP: Colleges often operate on a semester or quarter system during the school year. A semester is usually 15 or 16 weeks long; there are two semesters each year—fall and spring plus a shorter summer session. A quarter is usually 10–12 weeks long. There are three quarters (fall, winter, spring) plus a summer session in the academic year. You will also hear the word "term" used to describe the time during which classes are held. "It's midterm" or "end of the term" means it's the middle or end of the semester or quarter.

The schedule of classes will also provide information about assessment and placement testing; methods of enrolling—online, telephone, in person—and where to enroll; tuition and payment information and deadlines; financial aid and veterans benefits; as well as general information about topics such as faculty advising and where to go for service; locations, addresses, and phone numbers of the campus (or campuses) plus off-campus locations where classes are held; where to get an identification card and parking pass; and other important information that you'll find useful to have in one place.

TALK TO THE EXPERTS—ACADEMIC ADVISORS

Many community colleges require first-time students to see an academic advisor or to attend a group advisement session before they enroll in classes. To make it easy for you, walk-in advising is often available during registration and enrollment, so you won't need to make an appointment beforehand. If you're new to the system, an academic advisor will help you choose the curriculum and courses that suit your individual interests and goals.

Even if you aren't a new student, speaking with an advisor before enrolling in classes each semester is a good idea. Why? If you're a returning student, an advisor will make sure you're on track with your course selection and requirements.

Check with your college's advising and counseling office to see how you can get assistance from an academic advisor.

> **TIP:** Most community colleges offer a full range of student development courses and programs throughout the year on topics such as college survival, study skills, math anxiety, career development, and cultural orientation for international students. Courses are taught in classroom settings and are even available online. Ask an advisor what's available at your college.

Academic advisors will be available throughout the year to help you

✓ Decide what program of study you want to pursue—whether you want to enroll as a potential transfer student to a four-year school, study for a career-related degree, or pursue a certificate program.

✓ Understand the requirements for the program or major you have selected.

✓ Plan your schedule semester by semester to ensure you meet the requirements and plan ahead for advanced coursework.

✓ Decide on an appropriate course load to take; that is, the number of courses and credits that will work well with your personal schedule and other responsibilities. (You'll be considered a part-time student if you take 11 credits or less and full-time if you enroll for at least 12 credits.)

✓ Locate other campus resources, such as the career services center, veteran's office, office for students with disabilities, transfer center, or special programs for returning adults or women, which can also help you meet your needs.

> **TIP:** Community college services are designed for busy people. If you can't see an academic advisor in person during the semester, then check out the college's Web site for online advisement. You may find some answers quickly through an FAQ (Frequently Asked Questions) section or even be able to "chat" with an advisor online.

When you first enroll, the advisor you see may not belong to the specific academic department in which you may be interested, but he or she can get you started just by explaining the overall requirements. You also may not see the same advisor each time you need assistance. It will be helpful to you if you develop a relationship with one advisor who knows your situation and needs.

When you have chosen a major, you may be assigned to an advisor from that department. This person will be an invaluable guide to helping you sort out the often confusing array of requirements, what courses count and don't count toward graduation, and similar issues. Go see him or her on a regular basis!

Remember, academic advisors will be available to work with you during the year to make sure you succeed. Touching base with an advisor on a regular basis will keep you on track and help you avoid difficulties. Don't forget, it is your responsibility to contact the advisor!

TIP FOR PARENTS: If you want to speak with a college advisor or counselor along with your high school student, you can talk about anything freely BEFORE your student enrolls. Once the student is admitted and enrolls in coursework, however, the Family Educational Rights and Privacy Act (FERPA) affords students certain rights with respect to their education records. Then, you'll only be able to see your son's or daughter's records and discuss concerns with college staff with your child's consent.

VISIT THE CAREER CENTER NOW!

The career center will be another important source of information for you as you plan your educational program. Career counselors can help you identify your interests through self-assessment tests such as the Myers-Briggs test (a personality inventory that can help with career choice), or a Strong Skills/Interest Inventory (which focuses on work-related interests and skills for career assessment). You'll have one or two follow-up sessions with the counselor to help you understand your scores.

This type of testing is fun! It can help guide you to a field of study and potential job or career that might interest you. You'll be better able to select coursework and plan an entire program of study with this head start.

> *"Most students don't realize that the career center should be one of your first stops at the college, not the last one as you graduate or when you need a job. We have services that will help you throughout your college career to identify your skills, interests, and even a suitable major, if you're unsure about what you want to study. If you need a job on campus or are interested in cooperative education or internships, the career center is an excellent, but often overlooked, place to start your search."*
> — Jan Harris, Director of the Career Services Center, Community College of Philadelphia (Pennsylvania)

The career center is also a perfect place to explore how various majors relate to real jobs. Many colleges have online programs that allow you to search for an occupation, see what skills and knowledge are needed for the job, and what major(s) are best suited to help you gain those targeted skills and knowledge.

Jan Harris also notes that "Students sometimes have unrealistic ideas about majors and careers. One student I counseled was sure he wanted to be a geographer, but he hated math and science. He thought being a geographer just meant you got to travel around the world. He didn't realize that the very subjects he didn't want to study were the ones he needed for this career. He decided being a geographer wasn't for him."

GET ORIENTED!

Take advantage of new student orientation sessions, which first-time college students are often required to attend. They're recommended for all students, as are college success or survival skills courses. Dennis L. Bailey-Fougnier, Associate Dean of Student Development, Portland Community College (Oregon) says: "These sessions help students to learn and understand the nuts and bolts of college, such as what's a credit hour, how to put together a class schedule, how to log in to register, how to drop or add courses, how to figure out your grade point average, and how to understand a course outline (syllabus). They are really helpful to students. We try to reinforce the two-hour session with an online orientation that helps students review the information from the class. Students also receive a book, and during the semester, we email first-time students about important deadlines."

Be Admitted and Get Enrolled!

Now that you understand some of the basic information you'll need to apply to and be admitted to college, as well as some of the resources available to help you select your courses and develop a schedule, you'll be ready to fill out the paperwork for admissions, register, and enroll in your courses.

Remember you will need to register to take classes each semester and enroll in each course. You will be considered a full-time student if you take 12 credit hours a semester (usually 3 to 4 classes). You will be considered a part-time student if you take fewer than 12 credit hours a semester. Because community colleges are flexible, you can take the number of courses each semester that suits you.

Admissions & Registration Countdown

1. Get a college catalog with program requirements and course descriptions; obtain a schedule of classes. Check the college calendar for the semester (or quarter) start dates. Almost all colleges have this information available online as well as in print.

continued

Admissions & Registration Countdown (continued)

2. Contact the admissions (enrollment) office for an application and program information. You can download an application form from the community college Web site, email the admissions office for a form, pick up an application form in person, or call and have one mailed to you. Visit or speak with a counselor in the admissions office if you have concerns or questions.

3. Start the ball rolling with the financial aid office by contacting a counselor in that office even before you decide to apply for admission. Apply for financial aid. Explore scholarship opportunities and apply for those for which you are eligible.

4. Submit an admissions application (in print or online) with the one-time application fee to the college (usually the fee is minimal, but not refundable). *Make sure all the necessary documents, such as high school transcripts or immunization, have been submitted or are in hand.*

5. Speak with a counselor in testing and assessment (or the appropriate office at your community college) about assessment and placement tests (or if you may be exempt).

6. Check your mail for an acceptance letter and assessment and placement testing information.

7. Take any assessment or placement tests that are required.

8. See an academic advisor who can assist you with understanding academic requirements for various programs of study and help you select your courses and plan your schedule.

9. Register for classes in person, by telephone, or online. Check with the college about registration periods (also see the schedule of classes). Enroll as early as possible to ensure you get the class schedule and courses you want. Online enrollment, if available, sometimes starts a week or so earlier than in-person registration. You must register for each course! If you have any questions, contact the registration office (sometimes called the "Office of the

Registrar," who is the person who handles the registration process and all student records).

10. Pay your tuition and fees. Watch your mail for a tuition bill from the bursar's office (the office that collects fees for the college). Send full payment for your courses or participate in the college's payment plan.

> *"Remember to pay your bill on time! Whether you're paying yourself or getting financial aid, if the bill isn't paid, you risk losing the schedule of classes you so carefully constructed."*
> —Dale Smith, Associate Professor and Counselor, Office of Admissions, Westchester Community College (New York)

11. Receive a confirmation of your course schedule. Review it carefully to be sure that you have the courses, days, and times that you selected, and that you know where your classes will be held (that is, which campus if it is a multi-campus community college).

12. Get a student identification card. This card will allow you to use the facilities on campus.

13. Buy your books and get a parking pass. The campus bookstore will have a list of the texts that you will need for the courses for which you signed up.

14. Start class! Remember to keep consulting with academic advisors about courses you'll take in future semesters and if you run into any type of trouble—academic or personal.

15. If you're new to college, sign up for a college survival skills class. You'll learn a lot of useful study tips and get a good understanding of what you need to do in the classroom to be successful.

> **TIP:** If your community college has dorms, as some of them do, and you want to live on campus, be sure to apply early for space. By April, you might find only a waiting list for a space in the fall.

Registration for Non-Credit Courses

Registration for most *non-credit* courses offered through continuing education or workforce development is usually continuous throughout the fall, winter, spring, and summer sessions at community college. Most of the time, for non-credit courses, you will not need to go through the regular college admissions process, but colleges vary, so check out your college's requirements. Prior educational or work experience could be required to enroll in a particular course, especially those focused on enhancing work skills, preparing you for an entry-level job in a particular field or for licensing.

You should register as early as you can prior to the start of the class that interests you. Otherwise, it might be fully enrolled and you'll have to wait until the class is given again. Registration is usually on a first-come, first-served basis, and payment for the class must be completed before you'll be allowed to attend. Signing up is usually easy. You will be able to register in person, on the Web, by fax, or through the mail.

Remember that non-credit courses will not count toward a degree or transfer any credits to another institution. Some colleges co-list continuing education and workforce development courses as non-credit and for-credit courses so if you can choose what's best for you.

Students with Disabilities

Community colleges are committed to serving students with documented disabilities, and comply with Section 504 of the Rehabilitation Act of 1973, as amended by the Americans with Disabilities Act (ADA).

SNAPSHOT: Bobbie Page, a student at Community College of San Francisco, is legally blind. She returned to college to major in mathematics. "Take advantage of any services that are available. You will definitely benefit, not only in terms of your education, but also your self-esteem. The encouragement of my instructors and the special services—such as large-type texts, preferential seating in the classroom, and taking tests by computer, with additional time to take tests—have made all the difference in my being successful. It also helps to introduce yourself to your instructors before class starts. Tell them about your disability so they won't be surprised if you need special accommodations."

Disabilities cover a broad range of conditions, including, but not limited to, visual, hearing, and speech impairment; learning disabilities; psychological or psychiatric disorders; mobility loss; cerebral palsy; traumatic brain or closed head injury; and ADD/ADHD (Attention Deficit Disorder/Attention Deficit Hyperactivity Disorder). A wide range of services is available, such as assistive technology (special keyboards, speaking dictionaries, Braille listening devices, and so on), readers or scribes, interpreter services for the deaf and hard of hearing, and special arrangements for exams.

If you have a disability, you'll need to meet the same admissions criteria as other students and go through the same application process. *If you want to access supportive services, however, you will need to identify yourself to the college and be registered with the office that offers services to students with disabilities.* (Your college may call this office "Disabled Support Services," the "Office for Students with Disabilities," or some similar title.)

TIP: It takes some time to evaluate, process, and make arrangements for appropriate special accommodations. Colleges recommend starting your discussions early, with a 4–6 week lead time in your request for services.

Information about additional forms that you will need to file will be available online or through the office for students with disabilities. This office willl also provide you with counseling services and assistance in completing the forms.

You will need to supply appropriate documentation about the nature of your disability, treatment, prognosis, and other relevant material required by your college's guidelines to the office for students with disabilities. A counselor will also discuss your eligibility for service with you, evaluate the types of services you need, review your assessment test scores, and help you plan a schedule.

You'll need to fill out a request for services form that will help a counselor determine the type of classroom accommodations you will need. Once that is determined, you'll receive some form of documentation, sometimes called a letter of accommodations, to take to your instructors during the first or second week of classes to make arrangements for your authorized accommodations.

The U.S. Department of Education publishes an excellent pamphlet entitled, "Students with Disabilities: Preparing for Postsecondary Education, Know Your Rights and Responsibilities." It can be ordered online at www.edpubs.org. It is available on the Department's Web site at www.ed.gov/ocr/transition.html. It can also be ordered by writing to

    ED PUBS
    Education Publications Center
    U.S. Department of Education
    P.O. Box 1398
    Jessup, MD 20794-1398

By fax: 301-470-1244; by e-mail request: edpubs@inet.ed.gov, or by toll-free telephone at: 1-877-433-7827 (1-877-4-ED-PUBS). If 877 service is not yet available in your area, call 1-800-872-5327 (1-800-USA-LEARN). Those who use a telecommunications device for the deaf (TDD) or a teletypewriter (TTY), should call 1-877-576-7734.

International Students

Students from abroad come to pursue degrees, take intensive English language training, or a combination of the two. Although regulations about the entry of international students into U.S. institutions of higher education have tightened since 9/11, foreign-born students are still very much welcomed. In fact, the American Association of Community Colleges has an annual trip where it invites community college representatives to travel with them overseas to promote their institutions.

> **FAST FACT:** To serve international students, U.S. institutions of higher education have to be approved by the School Certification Branch of the Student and Exchange Visitor Program (SEVP). You can check the list of approved schools at www.ice.gov/graphics/sevis/pdf/ApprovedSchools/pdf at the U.S. Immigration and Custom Enforcement Web site.

Each community college has its own admissions requirements. You'll get the best specific information about a community college by going to its Web site first.

Most community colleges that accept overseas students spell out the requirements very clearly. They offer information about tuition (international students pay a higher tuition), available housing options (not every campus has dormitories), realistic costs of living, and suggestions about what to bring and what to expect in terms of adjusting to life in the United States.

Check to see if there is a special application for international students, which should be available online. If you have trouble finding the application, understanding admissions requirements, or completing the application, email the international student program or admissions office for assistance. It is very important to fill out the application completely and correctly; otherwise, your application and admission may be delayed.

TIP: The American Association of Community Colleges and Community Colleges-USA have a special Web site, www.cc-usa.org, for international students, with information about community colleges, entry requirements, virtual college fairs, and a search mechanism to find a specific college.

In most cases, you'll need documentation such as

✓ An application form from the community college you wish to attend.

✓ An I-20 Application form, available from the college. The I-20 form is a certificate of eligibility for non-immigrant student status.

✓ An official or certified copy of one of the following:

   Your secondary school diploma or certificate equivalent to a U.S. high school diploma. (Or, if you have not completed your secondary studies, an official letter from the institution stating when you will complete your studies.)

   Documentation of your attendance at a post-secondary college or university.

✓ Your most recent score on a language test, such as the Test of English as a Foreign Language (TOEFL), usually not more than two years old. If you are applying to the college only for intensive English Language studies, or if English is your native language, you will not need this test.

✓ Your Statement of Financial Support written in English and shown in U.S. dollars.

✓ A photocopy of your passport identification page.

All academic documents must be translated into English.

In addition, you may need to write a brief essay about why you want to study in the United States or at the particular college you have chosen.

Mail all of your information to the office specified by the college. The college will review your documents and, if you have met all the requirements, will mail you a SEVIS (Student and Exchange Visitor Information System) I-20 form. This is the official document you will need to receive an F-1 (student) visa from the U.S. Embassy in your country.

Your best source of information about how to apply for and receive a visa is the United States Embassy in your country of origin or from www.unitedstatesvisas.gov. Information is also available online from the Department of Immigration and Customs Enforcement Web site, www.ice.gov/graphics/sevis/students/index.htm. Don't forget that getting the appropriate documents from your proposed community college, as well as the visa, takes time. Plan ahead as much as you can.

When you arrive on campus, be sure to take advantage of the services that the college can offer you to make your transition to the American education system and way of life easier. Services will often include intensive English-as-a-Second Language courses and a comprehensive array of support services such as tutoring, counseling, basic skills courses, and career planning. You'll be asked to take an English language placement test to identify what level English course will be most beneficial for you.

TIP: Look for an International Center or International Students Program at your prospective community college for special assistance with immigration issues and for help with adjusting to the American culture and lifestyle.

Jean-Baptiste Sankara, an African student from Burkina Faso, is a recent graduate of Montgomery College (Maryland) who attends Rhode Island College. He advises: "Being a student from another country can be hard, but you have to realize that lots of help is available to you on campus if you ask for it. Getting involved in a club for international students or at the college's multicultural center is a good way to start learning about resources and creating a network of support. You'll meet a lot of other students, improve your English quickly, and start to form a circle of friends, which is important if you're here by yourself, as many of us are."

Find Out More

✦ www.salliemae.com (includes a special section on community colleges).

✦ For great advice about college majors and how they relate to over 450 occupations, go to www.myroad.com. You can match your strengths and interests with specific jobs.

✦ A good short book is *Fishing for a Major* from the Students Helping Students® series by Natavi Guides, Inc. New York: The Penguin Group, 2005. See also www.studentshelping students.com for online articles and advice on the same topic and other topics of interest.

✦ Advanced Placement Examinations—Check out www. collegeboard.com or www.petersons.com.

✦ International Baccalaureate Organization, www.ibo.org.

✦ CLEP (College-Level Examination Program)—The College Board (www.collegeboard.com), and Peterson's (www. petersons.com) offer detailed information about CLEP, online practice tests (for a fee), and information about colleges that grant CLEP credits; they have written study guides, *CLEP Success* (Peterson's) and *CLEP Official Study Guide* (College Board) that are available at your local bookstore.

✦ International students can search for community colleges, attend scheduled virtual college fairs, access excellent information about entry requirements, plan their costs and housing options at particular community colleges, and more, at www.cc-usa.org.

✦ International educational organizations such as the Institute for International Education (IIE) offer invaluable advice about every aspect of studying in the United States. See www.iie.org for more information. See also www.edupass.com for excellent information.

6

Keep the Costs Down: How Will I Afford It?

Many students, especially working adult students with assets, think they won't or don't qualify for financial assistance, so they don't research what might be available or apply. Almost everyone qualifies for something—a grant, a loan, a scholarship. I encourage students to look at all their aid options. Many of them are pleasantly surprised about the range of aid available for which they are eligible.

—Melissa Gregory, College Director of Student Financial Aid, Montgomery College (Maryland)

The cost of going to any college is rising, but community college is still a great bargain. That doesn't mean that it's always easy for students to find the funds to pay for college.

The good news is that financial aid is available from a number of state, federal, college, and private sources. You or your family can even get a tax break! With a combination of grants, loans, and scholarships from diverse sources, financial aid can substantially reduce your costs of attending community college.

There are lots of obstacles that might stand between you and going to community college, but money doesn't need to be one of them. Knowing what college costs, what types of financial aid are available, and how to get it will help you create a plan to be sure that community college will be affordable for you.

What Does Community College Really Cost?

Paying for college costs is a concern shared by everyone, especially if several members of a family are in college at the same time or are on the verge of entering college.

Figuring out what it will actually cost you to attend college means considering not just the obvious costs of tuition and fees (and room and board if you live on campus), but also other expenses that add up more quickly than you may think. You may not get a bill for these less visible costs, but your wallet will know that they are eating a hole in your pocket.

The general categories of costs you will need to consider are

✓ Tuition and fees

✓ Room and board

✓ Transportation

✓ Books and supplies

✓ Personal expenses

FAST FACT: The United States Department of Education estimates that in 2004-2005, the average price of attendance at a public two-year institution for a full-time student who was living off campus, but not with parents, was $11,707 ($2,000 in-district tuition; $5,926 in room and board; $2,849 in other expenses; and $932 for books and supplies.[1]

TUITION AND FEES

Tuition is the amount of money you pay for instruction in courses. It can be determined on the basis of the cost per credit hour and the number of credit hours in which you enroll, or it could be a flat fee charged by the college each semester or quarter.

For example, if you take 12 credit hours in a semester (this usually means 3 or 4 classes) and the cost per credit hour is $75, your cost for two semesters will be:

12 credit hours x $75/credit hour = $900 x 2 semesters=$1,800

Or, if your college charges a flat fee (one that is not based on credit hour) of $850 per semester, your cost for two semesters would be $1,700. Each college determines its own tuition costs and its method of charging tuition.

You may also be charged some additional fees each semester to cover costs such as student activities, use of technology, a student health services fee, or facilities usage. Sometimes, these charges are separate items and sometimes they are one consolidated fee for the term or the academic year.

Fees can add up, so be sure to include all fees when you are estimating the cost of attending for the year. And remember that you will need to calculate your tuition and fees for the *entire* year, including summer session if you take courses then.

TIP: Some states set a state-wide tuition rate for community colleges. Some community colleges have reciprocity agreements with other nearby community colleges (even those in neighboring states) so students who would not normally be considered residents can still pay the lower resident tuition.

Where you reside also determines your cost of tuition, as discussed briefly in Chapter 5. If you live in the service area covered by the college, you'll usually pay significantly less than if you are considered an out-of-district, out-of-state, or non-resident student. It's definitely worth making sure you are paying the lowest tuition rate possible by checking your residency status with the college.

There is often a different tuition and fee structure for non-credit courses, so be sure you are looking at the correct tuition and fee information when you check the college's Web site or ask about the cost of attendance.

> **TIP:** International students will almost always have to pay at least the out-of-state tuition and fees set by the college.

ROOM AND BOARD

The cost of room and board applies wherever you live, not just if you will be staying in a dorm. If you're living on campus, room refers to the cost of living in the dormitory. Board will be the cost of meals.

If you'll be living at home, you still may be contributing to family expenses, so consider these costs as part of your cost of attending college. If you have a family, chances are you'll have a monthly mortgage or rent payment and the usual bills associated with a home and children. If you're on your own and working, you know how much your mortgage or rent, utilities, and food expenses are.

You'll still need to consider these costs to make sure you're on target and don't come up short on living expenses.

Going to college might mean adjusting the amount of time you work and, consequently, the amount of your paycheck. Figuring out your living expenses and factoring in any reduction in income makes good sense. You won't want to find yourself strapped for cash or racking up credit card debt because you didn't plan ahead.

BOOKS AND SUPPLIES

No matter where you go to college, the cost of books and supplies comes as a big surprise to nearly everyone. Every course seems to have at least one required text that you just have to buy, and books never seem to get any cheaper. As noted above, at an average of over $900 per year for books and supplies, you'll need to be prepared to have enough money to purchase books for each class each semester.

TRAVEL

Most community college students are commuters, and some travel long distances to go to class. With rising gas prices and increasing costs of public transportation, travel can be a big part of your cost of attending college. Don't forget to factor this item into your budget.

PERSONAL/FAMILY-RELATED EXPENSES

Miscellaneous expenses can really add up fast and make a dent in your wallet and budget.

If you'll be commuting to campus, consider the costs of grabbing a cup of coffee and a meal on campus or off campus. Don't plan on bringing a sack lunch from home unless you're truly going to commit to having something prepared and ready to go before you need to dash out the door.

If you have children, consider the cost of child care as one of your potential expenses. You might have extended hours that require additional child-care coverage, or expenses associated with child care on campus.

Unraveling the Mystery of Financial Aid

Once you've got a grip on what your expenses will be, spending the time to research financial aid options, fill out those financial aid forms, or to write an essay for a scholarship application might seem more appealing.

FAST FACT: The College Board reports that "full-time students enrolled in public two-year colleges receive an average of $1,800 in grants and tax benefits from the federal government, state governments, institutions, and private sources."[2]

You'll want to consult with the experts in the financial aid office at your local community college (as well as with your high school counselor if you're in high school), understand types of available assistance, know how to apply for financial aid, and what additional options will be available to help you finance your education.

> **TIP:** Everyone, including adult students, should apply for financial aid. The vast majority of student aid programs do not have age restrictions. Although many awards are based on full-time attendance, part-time students can still qualify. There are scholarships, grants, and other funding through special programs for returning adults, single parents, displaced workers, individuals with disabilities, and other targeted groups. Don't automatically assume that because you are working or have assets, such as a house or savings, that you won't qualify for financial assistance.

GO SEE THE EXPERTS

If you're in high school, pay a visit to your guidance counselor for some advice about types of financial aid that will be available to you. Everyone can also benefit from an appointment with a counselor in the financial aid office at your local community college even *before* you apply. No one knows more about what's available and how you can access money to help with your education than the staff members in this office.

> **TIP:** Attending a financial aid workshop is one of the best ways to understand the options and process. Community college financial aid representatives conduct workshops on campus, at college fairs, local high schools, churches, associations, and in other venues. Look for nationwide financial aid days, such as College Goal Sunday, to help you get the information you need (for more information see www.collegegoalsundayusa.org)

Don't bypass an opportunity to get some financial support or find out if you qualify just because you don't understand the process, terms, or forms. No one new to the process automatically understands it all.

Even though a lot of information about financial aid is available online, it helps to sit down with a real person who can help you sort through your options and answer your questions. *Don't forget that the financial aid staff will also be the authority in making determinations about your financial aid eligibility.*

A counselor in the college's financial aid office can help you:

✓ Identify and apply for the right type of financial aid

✓ Answer questions about all types of aid—private, local, state, federal, and institutional (from the college)

✓ Understand eligibility requirements and help you complete forms

✓ Inform you about funding opportunities that you may not realize exist

TIP: Community college financial aid offices are extremely busy between May and October. January-April and mid-October-January are good times to make appointments with financial aid counselors.

Financial aid is a complex topic, so don't be shy about asking for help. Just don't wait until the last minute when everyone else needs answers too! Here are some questions to ask a financial aid counselor.

✓ What is the average total cost of attending college here? Have the tuition and fees (also room/board) increased recently and by how much? Do you anticipate another increase soon?

✓ What are the college deadlines for applying for financial aid? How do these differ from the federal government or state deadlines?

✔ How is my eligibility for federal financial aid determined? Does the institution have its own formula for determining financial aid eligibility?

✔ What types of scholarships are available through the college or other organizations? Is there a separate application or applications for this type of aid?

✔ How and when will I receive notification about financial aid awards?

✔ What will I need to do to maintain my financial aid?

✔ What types of tuition payment plans are available from the college?

Marga C. Fripp (Montgomery College, Maryland, Class of 2005) says, "Until I spoke with a financial aid counselor, I had no idea that there were so many opportunities for financial aid and scholarships. I received scholarships from the Coca-Cola Foundation, a New Century Scholar award, a Board of Trustees scholarship, and a privately endowed scholarship. I was able to take advantage of federal funding through the Pell grant and subsidized Stafford Loan. You have to do some work to access these funds, but it's really worth the time and effort, not only for the money, but also for the recognition and the added value to your resumé."

Understanding Available Types of Financial Aid

There are four major types of financial aid available from federal and state governments, colleges, and other institutions such as private foundations, companies, and organizations.

✔ **Grants** are funds awarded to students, most often on the basis of financial need, that do not need to be repaid. Grants are also given on the basis of other criteria, such as your interest in a special field of study or occupation or your status as a minority student.

✔ **Loans** are money borrowed from a lending institution such as a bank, a savings and loan, the federal government, or a private lender to help you pay for the cost of college. *Loans must be repaid with interest, and penalties exist if you do not repay on a timely basis.*

✓ **Work-Study** refers to a federally-funded employment program that lets you earn money to help pay the costs of your education. You'll be working for this money, so you don't need to repay it.

✓ **Scholarships** are usually awarded to students with some type of special qualification or distinction, such as academic, artistic, or athletic skill. They are often, but not always, based on merit or achievement. *Like grants, scholarships do not need to be repaid.*

Below you'll learn about some of the most common types of federal and state aid and scholarships available to community college students.

Federal Student Aid in Brief

It shouldn't be any surprise that Uncle Sam has the most money available for student financial aid. If you're undecided about whether or not to apply, think about this: Your tax dollars go to finance these programs, so if you are eligible, you are essentially tapping into a resource that you are helping to support.

✓ Many of these programs are *financial need-based programs* where your family's income, assets, and ability to contribute count in determining your eligibility to receive aid. It's worthwhile to fill out the forms and see if you're qualified. The Free Application for Federal Student Aid (FAFSA) is the application form you'll need to complete (see "What is FAFSA?" later in this chapter).

✓ Sources of funding and eligibility requirements for federal aid programs can change. If you don't qualify one year, don't assume that you don't qualify the next year. *The best source of information about all federal aid programs is the most recent copy of The Student's Guide to Federal Financial Aid*

Programs, available at www.studentaid.gov or by calling 1-800-433-3243).

✓ Most federal student aid funds can be used to pay for: (1) tuition and fees; (2) room and board (if applicable); (3) books and supplies; (4) computers; (5) transportation and some living expenses; and (6) dependent care. It's definitely worthwhile investigating.

✓ *Financial need is only one criterion that you will need to fulfill to be eligible for federal funding.* There are a number of educational and legal criteria that apply. Be sure to check with the financial aid office to understand what all the eligibility requirements are. (Other types of assistance, such as scholarships, have their own requirements).

The federal government also determines whether or not you are considered a *dependent* or *independent* student. This is an important factor in deciding how much you or your family must contribute to your education. If you are considered to be a dependent student, your parents' income and yours will both be considered.

You'll generally be considered independent by the federal government if you meet at least one of the following requirements:

1. Are 24 years of age by December 31st of the award year.
2. Are married or have legal dependents (other than a spouse) for whom you provide at least one-half their support.
3. Are an orphan or ward of the court.
4. Are a veteran of the U.S. Armed Forces.

It's best to check with the financial aid office if you have questions or special circumstances.

WHAT TYPES OF FEDERAL STUDENT AID EXIST?

Three major types of federal aid—grants, loans, and work-study—currently exist, each with its own requirements and merits. The section below identifies some of the most common federal programs. Keep in mind that eligibility requirements and amounts of assistance (and even the programs themselves) can change from year to year. Specific details about each type of assistance will be available from your college's financial aid office and also from www.studentaid.gov.

Federal Student Grants

Federal grants come in two categories: the *Pell Grant* and the *Federal Supplemental Educational Opportunity Grant* (FSEOG). Grants do not need to be repaid (unless you fail to continue to meet their criteria). They are usually disbursed to you through the college.

Pell Grants are one of the largest sources of funding for community college students. A Pell Grant is a needs-based grant, that is, one that takes into account your family's financial circumstances. The maximum Pell grant for the 2006–2007 award year will be $4,050 although the amount awarded each year could change. Part-time and full-time students can apply (part-time students will receive less funding than full-time students).

Federal Supplemental Educational Opportunity Grants (FSEOG) are for undergraduate students with *exceptional* financial need. Priority is given to students who receive Pell grants.

> **TIP:** The FSEOG grant is administered directly by the college you attend, so you will need to be aware of the college's financial aid deadlines, which are often earlier than the federal government's, for aid that it administers directly.

Unlike the Pell grant, which the government guarantees to each college for each eligible student, each participating college only receives a certain amount of FSEOG funds. *Once the money is gone, no more awards can be given for the year.*

The number of students who receive an FSEOG will depend on the availability of funds at that school. You can receive between $100 and $4,000 depending on your need, the funding level of your college, and your college's financial aid policies. Your college may or may not participate in this program.

Federal Loans

Sometimes, you or your parents may need to borrow some money to supplement any grants, scholarships, or work-study opportunities available to you. Loans that are provided by or guaranteed by the federal government are among the best available because they offer low interest rates and flexible payment plans.

TIP: Interest rates on federal student loans are usually lower than those from commercial lenders, such as banks. Interest rates on these federal loans, however, are also expected to go up 1.5 to 2.0 percent each year.

Remember that a loan, unlike a grant or scholarship, will need to be repaid—with interest and on time! You'll be paid directly by the college or credit will be applied to your account. Usually you'll receive at least two loan payments during the academic year.

Perkins Loans are available to students with exceptional financial need. In 2005-2006, undergraduate students could borrow up to $4,000 per year or a total of $20,000 under this program. There is no fee to take out this loan. One of the best features of this loan is that the government pays the interest while you are in college and for nine months after you graduate. You start paying the loan back after nine months, or if and when you withdraw from school or drop below half-time status. (This loan program is in danger of being cut from the federal budget).

Stafford Loans come in two forms—*subsidized* and *unsubsidized*—and are available to part-time and full-time students. Maximum loan amounts vary based on whether you are considered a dependent or independent student and by your status in school (that is, freshman, sophomore). You may apply for and receive both types of loans at the same time.

✓ **Subsidized Stafford Loans** are based on financial need and have low interest rates. They are called subsidized loans because the federal government pays the interest on the loan while you are in college and for a six-month grace period after you graduate. These loans are available at selected colleges and universities and come directly from the federal government.

✓ **Unsubsidized Stafford Loans** ARE NOT based on financial need. You can pay off the interest that accrues on the loan while you are in college, or you can have the interest added onto the principal loan amount and repay it when you graduate. These loans are available through private lenders through the Federal Family Education Loan Program. Your college will be able to help you identify private lenders.

FAST FACT: Stafford Loans require that you pay a fee of up to 4 percent of the loan. This fee is deducted from each loan disbursement so you will receive slightly less than the amount you borrow.

Federal PLUS Loans

Unlike the Perkins and Stafford Loans, which are loans to you, the student, the Federal PLUS Loan program is a loan to parents. It allows parents to borrow the full cost of attendance (an amount determined by the federal government) *minus* any aid received for dependent undergraduate students who are enrolled at least half-time in college. So if your cost of attendance is $3,000 and you're receiving $1,000 in other types of assistance, your parents could borrow $2,000.

Of course, you as the student must meet the general eligibility requirements for federal student aid. Your parents must also meet some criteria such as having a good credit history, must be citizens or eligible non-citizens, and not be in default on any federal student aid program. A co-signer might be necessary if their credit history is shaky.

Federal Work-Study Program

The goals of the Federal Work-Study Program are to help you earn money to pay for your educational expenses, promote community service, or engage you in work that is related to your course of study.

Under the Work-Study Program, you will hold a part-time job on campus at your college or off campus at a private not-for-profit organization, such as a local food bank, or a public agency, such as a government agency. Occasionally, placement may be with a for-profit employer, but usually your job must be related to your course of study.

> **TIP:** Working in the financial aid office at your college is a terrific way to become familiar with the available funding opportunities!

You'll earn at least the current minimum wage, if not more, and will normally be paid by the hour directly by your college. The amount you earn cannot exceed the amount of your Federal Work-Study award, so you can't work an unlimited amount of hours. The amount of your award depends on when you apply, your level of financial need, and the funding level of your school.

> **TIP:** Federal Work-Study is administered directly through your college so be sure to check out the college's deadlines for applying! There are usually more applicants than available jobs so apply early.

State Aid

Don't forget that your state will also be a valuable source of grants, loans, and scholarships. Sometimes, states are more generous than the federal government in how they calculate your income, so you may qualify for state aid even if you don't qualify for federal assistance. Usually, you must be a resident of the state to receive this type of student aid.

Common state offices that may offer assistance with identifying financial aid opportunities include

✓ State Department of Education

✓ State Financial Aid Office

✓ Department of Labor

✓ Office of Vocational Rehabilitation Services

✓ Department of Veterans Affairs

✓ Community Service Agency, especially for work-study opportunities

Because you will have completed the FAFSA form for federal aid, which many states accept, you will have taken at least one step toward potentially getting state aid. States also administer some federally funded aid programs that require the FAFSA form (see "What is FAFSA?," later in this chapter).

Scholarships and Grants

Scholarships and grants are available based on criteria such as academic merit, minority status, disabilities, and financial need. Many states also target scholarships, grants, and loans for specific occupations such as nursing, teaching, law enforcement, and other fields where there is a shortage.

Targeted Assistance Programs

States often administer state and federal funds for special programs such as dislocated worker grants for individuals who need retraining to re-enter the workforce, Individual Training Accounts through the Federal Workforce Investment Act to assist unemployed or underemployed individuals, and vocational rehabilitation programs aimed at individuals with disabilities. Many community colleges serve as the educational sites for these programs and can give you information about them.

Tuition Assistance Grant Programs

Tuition assistance grant programs that help defer these costs are also common at the state level. For example, New York State offers the Tuition Assistance Program Grant (TAP), which helps eligible New York residents pay tuition at approved schools in New York State. Depending on the academic year in which the student begins study, an annual TAP award can be up to $5,000. Because TAP is a grant, it does not have to be paid back.

Loan Forgiveness Programs

Also, check out loan-forgiveness programs for specific professions, especially nursing and teaching, and even for community service (loan-forgiveness programs are also available through the federal government).

Scholarships

Scholarships are one of the best types of financial aid because, like grants, they do not need to be repaid. Even if you don't qualify for federal or state aid, you might qualify for a scholarship. On the other hand, if you do get a scholarship, don't stop there. Continue to explore federal and state aid to round out your financial package.

SOURCES OF FUNDING

Scholarships and grants are available from a variety of sources including, but not limited to: private foundations, civic associations such as the Kiwanis Club or Rotary International Club, local businesses and national corporations, unions, community-based foundations, professional associations interested in supporting students entering a particular occupation such as accounting, business, or nursing. *There are many sources of information about scholarships, but one of the most comprehensive is www.fastweb.com.* You'll find additional resources under "Find Out More" at the end of the chapter.

ELIGIBILITY CRITERIA

Although many scholarships are based on academic merit, don't think you need to be a genius to get a scholarship! You can qualify for a scholarship in a number of ways. The specific criteria for a scholarship usually reflect the wishes of the person or organization that has provided the funding.

Eligibility criteria are very diverse, including recognition of achievements such as community service; athletic skill, musical ability, or another talent; low-income status; minority status; ethnic background, family ancestry or heritage, nationality, status as a non-traditional student, or first-generation college student; students with special needs or disabilities; or career goals. Even where you live or the high school you attended could make you eligible for a scholarship.

Scholarships are competitive, so you'll need to make an application. *Be sure to check the eligibility criteria and only apply for scholarships for which you are eligible.* You'll find out more about how to apply later in this chapter.

> **TIP:** International students are generally not eligible for federal or state financial aid, but may be eligible for many scholarships that do not have citizenship requirements.

THE COLLEGE CONNECTION

You may not realize it, but the college itself will often be a good source of scholarships. Check with your high school counselor and the college's Financial Aid Office (also their Web site) about scholarships available directly from or administered by the college.

Scholarships at community college are available for students who are pursuing a liberal arts or transfer program *and* for students in vocational and technical programs. So don't count yourself out because you are in a career-oriented area of study. Many corporations, unions, and associations have funded scholarships just for you.

Community colleges are very sensitive to the plight of part-time and working students and are more likely to have scholarships designated for them than other scholarship sources.

College Foundations

Many colleges have established foundations so that alumni, concerned citizens, and others can make donations to support the college and its students. Scholarships can range from several hundred dollars to full tuition and more. Donors love to help students, and scholarships are a perfect vehicle. Someone from your hometown might have designated a scholarship just for someone like you. You'll never know unless you ask.

Alumni Associations

Check out the college alumni association, which might also offer its own scholarships; some are especially designated for students whose parents attended the college.

Honors Programs

Many community college honors programs also offer scholarships to participating students, including part-time students. You'll need to qualify based on your grade point average and continue to meet the honors program requirements. But what could be better than being paid to study?

Other College Resources

If your college has a special office for returning adult students, individuals with disabilities, a women's center, and so forth, also check with them about scholarships and opportunities for special populations.

SCHOLARSHIPS ESPECIALLY FOR COMMUNITY COLLEGE STUDENTS

More and more prominent foundations are beginning to understand the important role that community colleges play in giving students an excellent start on their educational careers. That's good news for you because they've taken the lead in offering scholarships especially for community college students to help you achieve your goals.

Here are a few of the foundations and corporations that have put the spotlight on funding for community college students. Granted, these are very competitive scholarships, but you can and should aim high.

Jack Kent Cooke Foundation

The Jack Kent Cooke Foundation is a private independent foundation, established by the late Jack Kent Cooke, a prominent businessman, advocate for education, and philanthropist, to help individuals of exceptional promise reach their full potential through education.

The Foundation's Undergraduate Transfer Scholarship Program is the largest private initiative in U.S. history to help community college students pursue a four-year degree. Recipients who are attending or who have recently graduated from two-year colleges can receive scholarships to transfer to and complete their bachelor's degree at four-year colleges and universities.

> *"I'm not sure that even Mr. Cooke realized how much his scholarships change people's lives. Because of it, I am able to study at the college of my choice to pursue my dream of being an executive chef, open a restaurant, and eventually become a community college instructor. What's great is that this scholarship is open to anyone. I'm just an ordinary person, and I was amazed to be selected from so many terrific applicants."*
>
> —Athena Lapan, 2005 graduate of Central Piedmont Community College (North Carolina) and student at Johnson & Wales University (Charlotte, North Carolina campus)

Since 2004, when the Foundation designated these scholarships only for community college students, it has awarded 51 scholarships to a diverse group of students from 21 states and 8 countries. Approximately 60 percent of the Jack Kent Cooke scholars are women and 40 percent men from diverse ethnic and racial backgrounds. Scholars range in age from 19 to 53 years old. Another 54 community college scholars received awards in 2002 and 2003 when transfer students from four-year institutions were also included in the program, which has awarded a total of 160 scholarships.

Josh Wyner, Vice President for Programs, explains why the Foundation decided to focus exclusively on community college and two-year college students: "There are few private funds available to help community college students transfer to four-year colleges, although nearly 45 percent of all college students in the United States attend community college. We believe that the best students at community college are as good as the best students anywhere. Many talented community college students, however, might not consider going on to four-year schools or elite colleges because they lack financial resources. We don't want money to be an obstacle. The purpose of these transfer scholarships is to help open more doors so that community college students can achieve their educational goals and dreams."

SNAPSHOTS: At age 15, Alex San Pedro was homeless and on the street supporting himself. After overcoming alcoholism and other life hardships, he found his life-long passion in art and enrolled in Lane Community College Oregon, where he excelled academically while helping develop programs for homeless children. At 25, Alex was awarded the Jack Kent Cooke scholarship to study at Pratt Institute (New York), one of the finest art schools in the country. "I can go to school full time and concentrate on my studies. I'm hoping one day to open my own art gallery after getting a graduate degree at Yale University or Alfred University."

Linda V. Siegmann, 36, dreamed of being an accountant in high school, but life circumstances deferred her educational plans. She enrolled in Tulsa Community College (Oklahoma) and started pursuing her accounting degree. A member of the Quapaw tribe, she became actively involved in student groups, including the Native American Student Alliance, Phi Theta Kappa, and as a student member of several professional accounting groups. Linda has her eye on eventually getting an MBA, becoming a certified public accountant, and helping her tribe work on financial and taxation issues. "The Jack Kent Cooke Scholarship has made my dreams come true. It's opened so many doors and opportunities. It made me realize that there isn't anything I can't do."

Here are some specific details regarding the scholarship.

✓ Candidates must be nominated by their two-year institution in order to apply.
✓ Generally, 25 students are selected each year.
✓ The maximum available award per student is $30,000 per year.
✓ The award provides funding for tuition, room and board, books, and other required fees for the remainder of the Jack Kent Cooke Scholar's bachelor's degree, generally two years.

Academic achievement, financial need, exceptional character, and the ability of a student to become a leader and make the world a better place are some of the qualities the Foundation looks for in its scholars. *Check with your campus to see who your Jack Kent Cooke Scholarship representative is.*

Besides the funds to continue your education, the Foundation brings together scholars each year for special events, features scholars' progress and achievements on its Web site, www. jackkentcookefoundation.org, and in its publications, and offers continuing financial assistance through its program for graduate students.

Coca-Cola Two-Year Colleges Scholarship

The Coca-Cola Scholars Foundation is an example of a national-level corporate foundation scholarship opportunity for community college students. First- or second-year community college students from around the country may be nominated by their college to apply for the $1,000 Coca-Cola Two-Year Colleges Scholarships.

This scholarship focuses on students who have demonstrated academic success (minimum of 2.5 GPA) and who have completed 100 hours of community service within the previous twelve months. Students who are enrolled for at least two courses during the next term are eligible. Other eligibility criteria also apply. *See www. coca-colascholars.org for additional information.*

The Hispanic Scholarship Fund

Hispanic students form one of the largest populations served by community colleges. Formed in 1975, The Hispanic Scholarship Fund is the nation's leading organization supporting Hispanic higher education through scholarships and educational outreach.

Here are two programs that the Fund offers for community college students:

✓ The **High School Scholarship Program** is a national-level program for graduating high school seniors who plan to enroll full time in at a community college or a four-year institution. Award amounts range from $1,000 to $2,500. Eligibility requirements include citizenship or legal residency, Hispanic heritage, a 3.0 grade point average, full-time enrollment in an accredited college or university, and application for federal aid.

✓ The **Community College Transfer Scholarship Program** is available to part-time or full-time community college students of Hispanic heritage who plan to transfer to and enroll full time in a four-year institution the following academic year. Other eligibility criteria apply. Award amounts range from $1,000 to $2,500.

The Hispanic Scholarship Fund has also partnered with several major corporations—Coca-Cola, General Motors, Nissan, and Sallie Mae—to promote the transfer of community college students to four-year institutions. *See www.hsf.net for further details about all the scholarships described.*

Phi Theta Kappa

Phi Theta Kappa is the international honor society of the two-year college. It recognizes and encourages academic achievement of two-year college students, and provides them with opportunities for individual growth and development through participation in honors, leadership, service, and fellowship programming. As part of its commitment to community and two-year colleges, Phi Theta Kappa has developed several new and well-known programs to provide financial assistance and recognition to Phi Theta Kappa members.

LEADERS OF PROMISE

Phi Theta Kappa's newest initiative is the Society's first scholarship program *to be used during the time members are enrolled in their community colleges.* Here are some specifics regarding this program.

✓ A student must be a Phi Theta Kappa member in good standing and currently enrolled in a community college at the time of application.

✓ A total of 30 scholarships of $1,000 each will be awarded yearly based on applications submitted by members.

✓ Members must have a minimum 3.5 cumulative GPA at the time of application on all associate degree coursework.

✓ Part-time, full-time, and international students are eligible to apply.

FAST FACT: Phi Theta Kappa is the only two-year college honor society whose members are automatically nominated for inclusion in the National Dean's List, a prestigious publication of outstanding students in two-year, four-year, and graduate degree programs. Being on the National Dean's List means you're also eligible for a $1,000 scholarship. (See www.thenationaldeanslist.com.)

PHI THETA KAPPA TRANSFER SCHOLARSHIPS

Currently more than 600 colleges and universities, *including nearly half of the Ivy League schools,* in all 50 states, the District of Columbia, and Canada offer more than $36 million in transfer scholarships to Phi Theta Kappa members. The Phi Theta Kappa Web site, www.ptk.org has links to participating colleges and its eScholarship Directory has additional information about transfer scholarship opportunities.

ALL-USA ACADEMIC TEAM AND NEW CENTURY SCHOLARS AWARDS

Phi Theta Kappa also administers the *All-USA Academic Team Recognition Program,* which annually recognizes three 20-member

"Teams" of outstanding two-year college students, offering stipends of $2,500 each to the top 20 students. *All receive extensive national recognition through coverage in USA TODAY.*

The top-scoring applicant for the All-USA Academic Team in each state is named a *New Century Scholar* and receives a $2,000 scholarship. The New Century Scholars program is sponsored annually by the American Association of Community Colleges, The Coca-Cola Foundation, the Coca-Cola Scholars Foundation, and Phi Theta Kappa. Students nominated to the All-USA Academic Team are automatically named to the All-State Academic Team in participating states.

ADDITIONAL OPPORTUNITIES

Phi Theta Kappa also has other award opportunities available to eligible members including $100,000 through the Guisewhite Scholarship Program to help 20 qualifying Phi Theta Kappa members obtain their bachelor's degrees. *See their Web site, www.ptk.org, for further details and for links to other scholarship opportunities for community college students.*

MORE TRANSFER SCHOLARSHIPS— FOR THE FUTURE

Whether you plan to transfer to a public or private institution to get your baccalaureate degree, the cost is going to be substantially more than at community college, especially if you want to live on campus. Fortunately, community colleges and their four-year institutional partners also help ease the financial shock with transfer scholarships.

Criteria for eligibility and award vary by institution, but can include minimum number of credits transferring, grade point average, completion of an associate's degree, and other factors. Usually, you must have applied and been accepted to a four-year institution to be awarded a transfer scholarship.

Your community college financial aid office or transfer office should have a complete listing of what is available from institutions where your college has an articulation agreement (see Chapter 10 for more information about these agreements). Where no agreement is in place, you'll contact the four-year institution you wish to attend for transfer scholarship information.

Go for the Gold!

Now that you know what type of financial aid—federal, state, college-based, and private—might be available to you, you'll need some idea about how to go about applying for it. You'll learn below when and how to begin the process. Again, the college financial aid office will be a great place to get advice and start the process.

WHEN TO BEGIN THE PROCESS

The earlier the better! "Gee, I didn't realize I had to apply so soon" is a lament that financial aid staff hear too often. You can start researching financial aid possibilities as early as your freshman year in high school and, if you're an adult, just as soon as you get an inkling you might want to return to school.

Remember that you are always looking ahead to the next academic year when applying for financial aid. Early application ensures that you will be considered for *all* available forms of financial assistance and that you will get the best financial aid package possible. Often, you do not need to be admitted to the college to begin the financial aid application process (but you will have to be admitted and enrolled to receive the aid).

Here's some additional helpful information about financial aid deadlines:

✓ Deadlines vary for federal, institutional (college-based), and state aid. Colleges also have their own internal deadlines that may differ from both federal, state, and private funding deadlines.

✓ Many private scholarships require applications to be completed in October or November of the year *prior* to your entry into college.

✓ The federal government deadline for filing FAFSA is after January 1, but before June 30. The earlier you file, the better.

✓ On many campuses, applications filed by March 1 or 15 are given priority for all financial funding for the upcoming academic year. You'll still be considered for funding by the college after that date, but available funds may be running low.

Remember, it takes time to process financial aid applications, so the money doesn't appear as soon as you file your application. You don't want to end up enrolled in college with no funds to pay for it because you either missed a deadline or didn't understand the amount of time it takes to receive the funds.

> *"Money shouldn't be a stumbling block in getting your education. It's definitely worth the time it takes you to fill out the FAFSA form because the payoff can be tremendous in terms of financial aid available to you, especially if you want to move quickly toward completing your educational goals. Financial aid might allow you to work less, take more credits, and finish faster."*
>
> —Carol Mowbray, Director, Student Financial Aid and Support Services, College Financial Aid Office, Northern Virginia Community College

What is FAFSA?

FAFSA is the form that students love to hate. It's a necessary first step in the process of applying for almost any type of financial assistance.

FAFSA stands for *Free Application for Federal Student Aid*. If you want to apply for any type of federal student aid—grants, loans, or work-study—you must complete this form. Most states and many colleges also require or use this form for their non-federal financial aid programs. So by completing FAFSA, you have a triple advantage because you can apply for three levels of assistance: federal, state, and college.

FAFSA is important because the financial information that you supply will help determine the amount of money that you (or your family) will be expected to contribute to your college costs that year (Expected Family Contribution).

The difference between the Cost of Attendance (a standard amount determined by rules established by law, which may differ from your actual expenses) and the Expected Family Contribution equals your financial need.

FAST FAFSA FACTS

✓ This form is free and there is no charge to file it. You do not need to pay anyone or any service to obtain the form, complete it, or file it.

✓ You may complete a FAFSA form even if you have not yet been admitted to a college. You can file a print form or complete the process online via FAFSA on the Web (www.fafsa.ed.gov).

✓ File the form as soon after January 1 as possible, but not before January 1. The final filing date is usually June 30 of that same year. Filing by mid-March of the year you are planning to attend college will help maximize aid available to you.

✓ It takes between four to six weeks for your FAFSA form to be processed and for you to receive your Student Aid Report, which will show what you (or your family) is expected to contribute to your college education that year (Expected Family Contribution).

✓ FAFSA must be filed again EVERY YEAR to receive federal student aid because your financial circumstances and thus your eligibility may change.

This information from your FAFSA form will be used by the college to calculate your financial aid package, the combination of financial aid resources—grants, loans, work-study, scholarships—that the college financial aid office puts together to meet your individual needs as closely as possible.

The FASFA form is available in print from your high school counselor, the community college financial aid office, or from the federal government. *It is also available free online via most college Web sites and from www.fafsa.ed.gov. If you want to send your FAFSA form electronically, you can download FAFSA Express software to your computer.*

You can also do a test run of FAFSA on the Web by going to www.studentaid.gov and then to the FAFSA demonstration site. This is a good idea, as you will get a preview of the documentation that you (and your parents) will need to complete the form, such as annual tax return, earnings records, Social Security numbers, and so on, and of the amount of time you'll need to fill in the form.

> **TIP:** You may not be done with financial aid forms even after you complete FAFSA. Sometimes, colleges may require additional information and will ask you to complete their own forms or the College Scholarship Service (CSS) PROFILE (www.fafsa.com/profile.htm), another widely used form to help determine eligibility for financial aid. Scholarships often have their own special application forms.

It doesn't cost you anything but time (and some aggravation) to make the FAFSA application. Help in completing the form is available from your high school, the college financial aid office (which often has workshops for parents and students, sometimes at your local high school), and as well as online at www.fafsa.ed.gov.

FINANCIAL AID TIPS

Carol Mowbray, Director of Financial Aid and Student Support Services, Northern Virginia Community College, has these practical tips for students who are interested in obtaining financial aid.

1. Apply for financial aid as early as possible and apply for all forms of financial aid for which you are eligible. Don't assume that you are ineligible for financial aid. You may be overlooking significant financial help.

2. Read forms carefully and pay attention to detail when you are completing forms, especially FAFSA. Mistakes cost you time and can cost you money.

3. Make sure that your name matches exactly the way your name is stated on your Social Security card, especially for the FAFSA documents. Lack of a match can delay your application.

4. Open your mail (print or electronic)! Follow up and respond to requests, whether they're from the government or from the community college. For example, if you complete FAFSA and there is a mistake or additional information is needed, you need to respond quickly.

5. Read the information in your award letter carefully so you understand what you need to do to maintain your grant, loan, or scholarship. For federal funds, you must maintain satisfactory academic progress or you may not qualify for more financial aid.

6. Be sure to tell your college whether or not you are accepting some or all of the financial aid package they offer you.

7. CASH YOUR CHECK. Most checks are good for 60 days or they are cancelled. After tuition is paid to the institution, you may still have some funds available. If you don't claim them or use them, especially federal funds, they may disappear at the end of the fiscal year.

8. Be organized. Keep copies of all the financial aid applications and correspondence.

9. Keep your college updated about change of residential address or change of email address. If you move, the college needs to know so information goes to the right place.

10. Think about financial aid in terms of your overall educational and career plans. If you know that you plan to go on to a four-year college or university, think about how much money you'll need not only at community college, but also for the next several years.

What You Can Get in Your Package

You might be eligible to receive assistance in several ways—grants, loans, work-study, and scholarships. Receiving one form of assistance doesn't necessarily preclude you from receiving another, but they will all be balanced together to form your financial aid package.

How much you receive depends on factors such as:

✓ Cost of attending the college

✓ Your financial need

✓ Availability of funds

✓ Your college's aid policies and federal and state financial aid programs in which they participate

✓ The number of students who request or need financial assistance

The financial aid office will use federal and state guidelines to examine your eligibility for federal, state, and institutional aid programs based on your financial need. Staff will check your eligibility for grants and scholarships first, followed by your eligibility for the Federal Work-Study program or student loans. Scholarships from outside sources are also considered. The final product will be your financial aid package.

When the financial aid office has determined what your financial aid package will be, you will receive an award letter. It will tell you:

✓ The amount of your financial need

✓ How your financial need was determined

✓ Types and amounts of aid offered

✓ How and when you will receive the funds

✓ Student employment conditions if you are in a work-study program

✓ The terms and conditions of the offer, such as the number of credit hours you must take each semester or quarter to remain eligible or the academic requirements you must meet to maintain your funding

✓ Whether or not the award is subject to availability of funds

It's important to understand that your financial aid package may not cover all of your financial need, but it will go a long way to making college more affordable for you. You also can accept some or all of the financial aid package. For example, if you decide that you'd rather not have a loan, you can decline that portion of the package. Whatever you decide to accept or decline, you do need to inform the college!

APPLYING FOR SCHOLARSHIPS

Scholarships can take a bit of work to get, but they will reward you with funds that don't need to be repaid, recognition, and often the opportunity to participate in special programs or events designated for scholarship winners.

Scholarship forms vary in complexity. Some require only completion of a short form. Others that are very competitive require more thought and imagination to help you distinguish yourself from the crowd.

For example, for scholarships that are based on special talents, skills, community service, and so on, you may need to write an essay about yourself, your experience, why you need or merit the scholarship, or show a sample of your creative work.

> **FAST FACT:** Scholarships can affect the amount of funding you receive from the federal or state government. Your financial counselor at the community college will help construct your financial aid package so that you can leverage all sources of aid to your benefit.

Here's how to apply for a scholarship:

1. Check out scholarship opportunities online, at your high school or community college financial aid office, or through publications available at your local library. Be creative! Scholarships exist for the most unlikely reasons and can be found in unlikely places.

> **TIP:** Watch out for scholarship scams! For example, if someone online, on the phone, or through the mail claims that you've won a scholarship or that they can guarantee a scholarship if you'll just pay a small fee, run the other way! There's a reason it sounds too good to be true, and the person getting the money won't be you! You don't have to pay an individual or a service to find a scholarship. There's plenty of free information available.

2. Get the names, addresses and applications for scholarships from your high school counselor, community college financial aid office, or directly from the scholarship funder by writing or calling them. Sometimes, your college will have one scholarship application form that covers the ones available

directly through it. Other times, funders might have their own special applications.

3. Review the application deadlines and eligibility criteria carefully. If you're unsure about your eligibility, check with the funder or the financial aid office. *Only apply for scholarships for which you are eligible so you won't be disappointed.*

4. If you need a recommendation or have to be nominated, choose individuals who know you well and who can write knowledgeably and positively about you. Some scholarships require nominations from your school.

5. Fill out the application carefully and completely. Have someone else read your application to be sure your grammar and spelling are correct.

6. Send out applications on time! Missing a deadline means you're missing out on an opportunity!

7. Receive your award letter. If you receive a scholarship, sometimes checks are co-payable to you and your college, and the funds will be applied to your student account for eligible costs.

8. Be sure to thank the scholarship donor!

9. Stay on course! Even though you won't have to repay the money, you might have to continue to meet certain criteria, such as maintaining a certain grade point average or performing community service, to keep the scholarship.

Still Short? Here's What to Do!

Financing your college education will require some creativity on your part. In addition to exploring available loans, grants, work-study opportunities, and scholarships, there are other ways to offset some of the costs of college: community service, employer assistance, military service or veteran's benefits, and some tax breaks from the IRS.

COMMUNITY SERVICE

Turn your desire to help others into an opportunity to attain your own educational goals. For example, AmeriCorps offers students a great way to lend a hand while earning a modest stipend and funds for college (www.americorps.org; tel. 202-606-5000). Another federal program, Learn and Serve, offers competitive college scholarships to high school students who have demonstrated leadership while participating in service projects (www.learnandserve.org; tel. 202-606-5000).

SNAPSHOT: Deborah Smith, a 50-plus mother of seven served as an AmeriCorps volunteer with Habitat for Humanity for two years. "I wasn't able to transfer the nearly $10,000 worth of tuition to one of my children or grandchildren so I decided to go to college myself. I enrolled in Kirtland Community College (Michigan) and had many costs of college covered by the AmeriCorps educational funds. I was also fortunate to have a wonderful honors scholarship at Kirtland. At the same time I studied at Kirtland, I was also enrolled in Madonna College. Between the two colleges, I was able to access financial aid—Pell grants and some state grants to help me along."

EMPLOYER ASSISTANCE

Many employers offer tuition assistance, often based on you achieving a passing grade, to encourage employees to continue or complete their education. This type of underwriting can be for work-related courses through short-term workforce development programs or for longer-term degree- and certificate-related study.

TIP: Community colleges work closely with local unions on apprenticeship programs in skilled trades such as building construction, plumbing, heating and air conditioning, electrical work, and printing. You can earn a salary while you learn on the job and the union will pay for your educational expenses.

It's definitely worthwhile to make a trip to the human resources office of your employer or your parents' employer to check on their policies. If an employer is willing to invest in you and your education, why not take advantage of the opportunity and financial assistance? It's a benefit to you that will keep paying in terms of promotions, higher pay, or, eventually, a better job.

SNAPSHOT: Keith Armstrong, a detective in Jersey City, New Jersey, who attends Hudson County Community College says, "My employer, the Jersey City Police Department, feels that an educated member of the force is an asset to the department and the community so they encourage us to pursue an education. To back that up, they also pay for our education. You can't beat that as an incentive."

JUST PLAIN WORK—BUT NOT TOO MUCH!

Of course, you may already be working part time or full time when you decide to enroll in community college. You'll need to find a balance of the two that's right for you, as it's hard to juggle a job and school.

If you need to look for a job to help meet expenses, choose work related to your proposed course of study. Explore cooperative education options, where you'll learn and earn at the same time (see Chapter 9). You'll build your resume with your on-the-job experience, make valuable contacts for future jobs, and find out whether that field is really for you. You'll still be ahead on the earning curve for the future.

CONSIDER A PRIVATE LOAN

Nobody wants to graduate with a load of debt. Sometimes, however, taking that loan may be necessary. It may also be the quickest way to reach your goal of graduating and starting a career. With discipline, you can pay off the loan quickly. You may want to be sure that you have exhausted every other possible source of aid before taking out a loan with a private lender.

> **TIP:** Many types of lenders—banks, credit unions, savings and loans, consumer finance companies—offer loans for education. Usually, private loans will have higher interest rates and fees than federal loan programs. Your community college will usually have a list of preferred lenders, that is, lenders that are recommended because they will treat you well, have fair rates, are reliable, and have an ongoing relationship with the college.

One of the nation's largest providers of college financial aid is The SLM Corporation, commonly known as Sallie Mae. Among the many types of loans available, it has two private loan programs targeted specifically for community college students, which provide funds beyond what federal programs offer.

✓ Community College Loan [SM] offers credit-based loans for students enrolled in associate degree programs and in Title IV (federal financial aid) eligible certificate programs.

✓ The Continuing Education Loan [SM] provides loans for students who are not seeking degrees, especially for those in professional or technical non-degree or certificate programs. Part-time students seeking degrees may also apply.

See www.salliemae.com/apply/borrowing/commcoll.html for additional information about eligibility, loan amounts, and terms of the Community College Loan and www.salliemae.com/apply/borrowing/continuinged.html for the Continuing Education loan.

Like all loans, you need to repay all private loans according to the terms to which you agreed or you'll be dodging collection agencies.

THE MILITARY OPTION

Don't overlook benefits that might be due to you for your service to the country! Check with the college about educational benefits available to military personnel, veterans, or their dependents.

If you want to join the service, you can either attend college first or perform your service and then get assistance to pay for your education. Remember that you will have an obligation to serve once you complete your studies.

If you want to attend college first, check out the ROTC (Reserve Officers Training Corps). You might be eligible for merit-based scholarships in return for a commitment to serve once you graduate. If you're already serving in the Reserves, your service can also make you eligible for educational benefits. Military-based associations and foundations, such as the Military Officers Association of America, the Marine Scholarship Foundation, or the Navy League, also offer scholarships to students.

See www.gibill.va.gov for an overview of educational benefits available to veterans. See www.todaysmilitary.gov for information about the educational benefits associated with joining the service and ROTC.

TIP: Remember that your community college also may have creative ways to help you pay for tuition and other bills, such as a monthly payment plan or an installment payment plan. Check with your financial aid office to see what's available.

GET A BREAK! A TAX BREAK, THAT IS

Education pays in more than one way. Even though you're spending a bundle on tuition, fees, and possibly room and board, you or your family can get some of it back if you qualify for tax breaks provided by the Internal Revenue Service.

Tax breaks take the form of a credit or a deduction. Tax credits are subtracted from the tax your family owes. Tax deductions are subtracted from your taxable income. For example, if you qualify for a $1,000 tax credit, you save $1,000 no matter in which tax bracket you are. If you qualify for a $1,000 deduction, only a certain portion of that $1,000 will be saved, depending on your tax bracket.

The government also offers deductions for student loan interest application to federal and non-federal loans.

> **TIP:** Your best source of information about tax breaks is the Internal Revenue Service (www.irs.gov). See especially IRS Publication 970, *Tax Benefits for Higher Education*, which explains these credits and other tax benefits. You can find out more by calling the IRS at 1-800-829-1040. TTY callers can call 1-800-829-4059.

GET CREDIT FOR LEARNING

You or your family may be eligible to receive a tax credit through *the Hope Scholarship Tax Credit* or the *Lifetime Learning Credit.*

The Hope Scholarship Tax Credit is available to students and parents of dependent students for the first two years of post-secondary education only.

You'll earn a credit of up to $1,500 in qualified expenses for each eligible student. The student must be pursuing an undergraduate degree or another recognized educational credential, and must be enrolled at least half-time for at least one academic period during the year.

A Lifetime Learning Credit is available to students and parents of dependent students for all years of post-secondary education (not just the first two as with the Hope Credit) and for courses to acquire or improve job skills. In other words, the student does not need to be pursuing a degree or another educational credential to be eligible to receive this credit. You just need to be enrolled in one or more courses.

- ✓ You can earn up to $2,000 credit per tax return.
- ✓ There is no limit on the number of years for which you can claim a Lifetime Learning Credit for the same student's expenses.

Qualified expenses for both types of credits include tuition and enrollment fees, but usually not the cost of books, student activities, room and board, or other types of living expenses. Income limitations and filing qualifications apply, so be sure to check these limitations at www.irs.gov.

Find Out More

✦ These comprehensive sites have excellent planning information and tools as well as links to federal, state, and private sources of funding: www.finaid.org and www.community. collegeanswer.com.

✦ Barbara Wagner. *Paying for College: Get an Education without Breaking the Bank!* Indianapolis: John Wiley & Sons. 2003.

✦ Gen Tanabe, Kelly Tanabe, and Terry Smith. *501 Ways for Adults Students to Pay for College: Going Back to School without Going Broke.* Supercollege, LLC. 2004. See also their Web site, www.supercollege.com.

✦ The Federal Student Aid Information Center (FSAIC) is available to answer questions about federal aid. Toll-free contact numbers are Federal Student Aid Information Center (FSAIC) 1-800-4-FED-AID (1-800-433-3243); TTY users (for the hearing-impaired) can call 1-800-730-8913. Callers in locations without access to 800 numbers may call 1-319-337-5665 (this is not a toll-free number).

✦ www.fafsa.ed.gov is the official federal government site for the FAFSA form and information (www.fafsa.com is NOT the federal site). You may also call 1-800-433-3243 for forms and additional information.

✦ www.studentaid.ed.gov provides a very comprehensive online guide to all forms of federal student aid and planning information in English and Spanish. You can also access *The Student Guide to Federal Financial Aid Programs* and *Funding Your Education* in English and Spanish.

✦ A good place to start in researching state aid is your state's Higher Education Agency. The U.S. Department of Education database at www.studentaid.ed.gov has contact information and Web addresses.

✦ *The College Board Scholarship Handbook* by College Board and *Peterson's Scholarships, Grants & Prizes* by Thomson's Peterson are updated annually and are available in bookstores and libraries.

- ✦ www.fastweb.com has the largest database of scholarships and offers free, personalized scholarship information and searches.

- ✦ Coca-Cola Scholars Foundation
  1-800-306-COKE
  www.coca-colascholars.org

- ✦ Hispanic Scholarship Fund, Headquarters
  1-877-HSF-INFO (1-877-473-4636)
  www.hsf.net

- ✦ Jack Kent Cooke Foundation
  703-723-8030
  www.jackkentcookefoundation.org

- ✦ Phi Theta Kappa
  601-984-3504
  www.ptk.org

7

Know the Ropes: What Can I Expect in Community College Classes?

> " *At community college, we're dedicated to providing the best context possible for you to learn plus a support network geared to your success. Community colleges are student-centered. It's this philosophy that makes a difference for our students, and that lets us transform lives every day.* "
>
> —Dr. Stephen M. Curtis, President, Community College of Philadelphia, Pennsylvania

One of the best features of community college is that the college is there for *you*. It's totally focused on you as the student and providing you with opportunities and resources for your success.

Because community college will be new to you, you may be concerned about who your instructors and classmates will be, where your classes will take place, what will be expected of you in class, and how much time going to community college will require.

This chapter will answer those questions. You'll have to do a lot more than you did in high school because you'll be in charge of your education. You'll find the courses to be challenging. Knowing what to expect, as well as understanding the dedication of your professors to the teaching and learning process, will help you succeed.

What Can I Expect in the Classroom?

You'll find a wealth of knowledge and experience in the classroom in the individuals who will be your instructors. They are dedicated to teaching and to creating an excellent learning environment that will help you succeed. In addition, you'll benefit from small class sizes, your classmates' diverse backgrounds, and the varied settings in which classes are conducted.

WHO WILL BE MY INSTRUCTORS?

Unlike four-year institutions, where many freshman and sophomore (first and second year) courses are taught by teaching assistants who are graduate students themselves, community colleges pride themselves on having only faculty members in the classroom.

Faculty members are the professionals who will be teaching you at college. You may hear them referred to by different titles that reflect their academic ranks—that is, their level of experience, time in the position, and academic background. Instructor (beginning level), assistant professor, associate professor, and full professor (highest level) are the most common ranks. The terms "instructor," "professor," or "faculty" are also used as general terms to refer to the individuals who teach courses at the college without necessarily referring to rank.

Your courses may be taught by full-time or adjunct faculty members. For full-time faculty members, teaching at the community college is their main professional activity. They have extensive training and knowledge in their special field of expertise, and keep up to date through professional associations, conferences, and other professional training opportunities.

Adjuncts, as they are commonly known, usually teach part time, that is, one or two courses during a semester at a college. They may also teach at other colleges in the area or hold full-time jobs in other professions. Adjuncts are often hired to teach because they are working in the field or industry, are experts in their field, and have the most current knowledge to offer. You'll find many adjuncts teaching in non-credit continuing education and work-force development programs as well as in for-credit courses.

Many community colleges require that both part-time and full-time faculty members who are teaching for-credit courses have a master's degree. Many faculty in community colleges also have a PhD. So don't worry: Your instructors will be first-rate on all counts.

To give you an idea of the experience and diversity of faculty at community colleges, here are some snapshots:

✓ Frederick A. Howell is director of the Computer Publishing and Printing Department at the Horace S. Gudelsky Institute for Technical Education at Montgomery College in Maryland. He has been teaching there since 1984 and is a full professor. He has two master's degrees, one in special education and one in vocational education. His experience comes from his many years of working in his family's printing business, as well as from starting and running his own printing business.

✓ Cathie Seidman is a former criminal prosecutor who, after teaching one semester at a four-year college, decided her real place was not before a judge, but in front of a classroom. Since 2001, she has taught full time in the Criminal Justice Department at Hudson County Community College in New Jersey and is a tenured faculty member. She has a bachelor's degree, a law degree, and has completed 30 credits toward a master's degree in Criminal Justice at Rutgers University, where she also teaches several graduate courses. Many of her students are studying to become police officers or fire-fighters. Others already work in these professions and are studying to advance their careers in criminal justice.

✓ Jeffrey Wright is a graduate of the Aviation Maintenance Technology program at Cincinnati State Technical and Community College (Ohio). He began teaching as an adjunct instructor there and now teaches full time. He has also worked for firms such as ComAir Airlines, General Electric, and Airborne Express in many capacities ranging from aircraft mechanic to aircraft inspector to manager of maintenance control. He has worked for Lockheed Martin as a technical writer and still does so part time. He completed his bachelor's degree at Embry-Riddle Aeronautical University and is now studying there for his master's degree.

✓ Dancer, teacher, and choreographer Kathleen Harty Gray has been an adjunct instructor in modern dance at Northern Virginia Community College (NVCC) since1995. She teaches in the Division of Visual & Performing Arts & Public Services and in the Continuing Education Program. Ms. Gray earned her Bachelor of Science degree in Dance at the renowned Julliard School, where she studied with dance legends Martha Graham, José Limón, and Anthony Tudor. She also holds a master's degree in education from the University of Virginia. Previously, she was a tenured professor at Mary Washington College (Virginia); she has also taught in many four-year colleges and dance studios throughout the Washington D.C. area. NVCC is now home to her dance company, KHGDT, one of the longest-standing modern dance companies in the area. Her company offers many programs in high schools and senior citizens centers. She has also performed and taught in Italy, China, Russia, and Japan.

No matter what their backgrounds, faculty members at community colleges are there because they love to teach. Although many of them also conduct research and publish articles and books, as do their counterparts at four-year colleges and universities, for community college faculty, teaching in the classroom is their primary purpose. Their main focus is on you and your success. To this end, oftentimes, faculty members will also serve as academic advisors who will help guide you through your academic work. They also work with students in community service projects, as club sponsors, on campus publications, and in many other extracurricular activities[1]

Dr. Anita Schwartz, who holds a PhD in anthropology from New York University, has taught at Nassau Community College (New York) on Long Island for nearly 30 years. She explains why she enjoys her work: "It's still challenging because I keep making changes as my students change. I still feel that I make a tremendous difference in the way my students begin to think and that's powerful. I can make a difference in who they are and who they become. My colleagues come from many different backgrounds;

some hold degrees from Ivy League schools such as Harvard and Yale. We're all united by the fact that we love to teach and believe in the mission of community colleges."

How Large Will My Classes Be?

At community college, you won't be faced with an enormous lecture hall filled with 100 or more students. Even at large community college campuses, class sizes are smaller, typically between 25 and 40 students. Even laboratory sessions will be small so students can receive individual attention. Basic skills courses usually have 15-20 students to allow for enhanced individual attention. Small class sizes means you'll have a better opportunity to get to know your professors, interact with many of your classmates, and participate in class, *if* you take the opportunity to do so.

Dr. Stephen M. Curtis, President of Community College of Philadelphia, emphasizes the importance of small class size in the learning experience at community college: "Even with 20,000 students taking credit-bearing courses a semester and all the students who take non-credit courses, we try to maintain a maximum class size of 33. Adults returning to school often like and need this type of smaller learning environment. It also suits students coming directly from high school who need more structure and personalized attention than a four-year institution can provide."

Who Will Be in My Classes?

As discussed in Chapter 2, you'll find a rich and often surprising diversity of students at your college and as your classmates.

One of the most surprising features to students is the diversity of age range and life and work experiences of community college students. In your class, you may find a mix of high school students who are taking some courses at the community college, recent high school graduates, working adults ranging from factory workers to professionals, stay-at-home moms, and retired adults. Sometimes, daytime classes have more traditional-age college students who may be able to attend class on a full-time basis. Evening classes often tend to serve more working adults who are employed part or full time.

As an older student, you might experience some anxiety about entering college for the first time, or returning to the classroom after an absence. Often, older students are concerned about the age difference with younger students. Don't worry. You won't be the only one.

Connie Murray, who has taught political science for over 15 years in several New Jersey community colleges, says "I've had classes with students whose ages range from 22 to 70 years old. One of my best students, Max, was in his eighties. He was a serious student taking courses for credit. Many nontraditional-age students are afraid that the younger students won't relate to them and vice versa. I've found that younger students aren't reluctant to become friends and usually find that the older students add a lot to the classroom experience."

SNAPSHOT: Roy R. Gordon (Montgomery College, Maryland, Class of 2005) says: "When I first decided to go back, I was terrified. Here I am a man in my late forties walking into a classroom with potentially brighter and younger students. I just hoped that I wouldn't embarrass myself. I'm very confident about myself in my work environment, but I was going back to study subjects I hadn't thought about in years. It's very anxiety producing at first. If you fail, you've done it on stage, so to speak, in front of a group of people. Eventually, you realize everyone's anxious about being there—no matter what age—and you begin to relax and learn from each other."

Older students bring the voice of experience into the classroom and add depth and richness to it. Dr. Frederick Teti, who holds a bachelor's degree from Yale University and a PhD from University of California, Berkeley, has taught mathematics at Community College of San Francisco since 1995. He observes: "If you're a younger student, finding someone older who is a good role model can be very helpful. They'll motivate you, keep you on track, and prevent you from falling into unproductive modes of doing things."

No matter where you go to college, you're bound to meet new people with different opinions, experiences, and backgrounds. You'll be able to learn as much from them as they will learn from you. Some will develop into friends and become your support network (See Chapter 8).

WHERE WILL MY CLASSES BE HELD?

Your classroom at community college isn't limited to the campus. Whereas it might be a classroom on the main or regional campus, it could also be a shopping center where the college has opened up a site, the community itself when you take a class field trip to another part of town or to a museum, an on-campus laboratory, or a worksite where you have a cooperative education, internship placement, service learning project, or a work-study experience (See Chapter 9 for more information about cooperative education, internships, and service learning; see Chapter 5 for work-study).

Special Facilities

In many vocational and technology programs especially, your classroom will resemble the environment in which you will be working when you will have a job.

Ed Roberts, who is dean of Montgomery College's Homer S. Gudelsky Institute for Technical Education describes their facilities: "We have an HVAC lab with donated up-to-date heating and air conditioning units from local suppliers, an automotive lab with cars and state-of-the-art equipment from manufacturers such as Ford and Subaru, a framed-out house for building and construction students, a computer lab where students learn how to diagnose problems and repair units, and a digital printing and publishing lab with up-to-date equipment donated from the industry. We work hard with industry to ensure that students are trained on the most advanced equipment and under circumstances that simulate a real work environment."

Aviation maintenance technology students at Cincinnati State Technical and Community College take the majority of their courses at a special facility located several miles from the main campus. It has $12 million worth of aeronautical equipment, including seven airplanes. Almost all instruction—technical and academic—occurs at this site. Professors teaching English, speech, and other required general education courses come on site to teach their courses, so students in the program may take only a few courses at the main campus.

In the Community

Some programs, such as nursing, place you in a hospital, community health center, or other clinical setting right away. You'll still have lectures and laboratories on campus, but you'll spend some time each week learning in work settings with professional nurses.

Amanda Alkins, a 21-year-old registered nursing student at Community College of Philadelphia started her clinical work at a hospital her first semester. "I was really surprised how fast we actually started working and learning in the hospital. Two days a week, we spent six hours a day at a hospital for the whole semester. Basically, we learned how to do a nurse's job: checking vital signs, preparing medications, cleaning and assisting patients under the supervision of the instructor. The second semester, we were organized into teams and learned how to manage other people and delegate work. This was combined with two hours of hands-on laboratory work at the college plus lectures and a one-hour seminar. In the lab, I learned proper techniques for doing procedures such as inserting catheters and taking vital signs, as well as sterilization procedures.

"This year, the setting will be more in the community—at schools, in patients' homes, at health fairs and screenings for one semester—and then another hospital placement. My final placement will be in a long-term care facility like a nursing home and another hospital. The types of hospital placements vary from small ones to large ones in different areas of the city.

"It's great because you really learn what you need to be a good nurse—not just the technical skills, but skills and confidence that you need to work well with patients."

Distance Learning

Your classroom could even be your own home or anywhere you have access to a computer, television, or radio. Community colleges have been leaders in pioneering distance learning, that is, learning taking place through a medium such as the Internet, satellite, video teleconferencing, video tapes, televised classes, or even radio broadcasts from the college's station.

Distance learning courses are popular with many community college students. They allow you to complete a course at your own pace (within a designated time frame) and to structure your own classroom experience. These courses do have assignments, examinations, and timetables for submission of materials, so they require discipline and good study habits for you to be successful.

With videocassettes, for example, you'll have the opportunity to watch a class on tape and review material at your own pace. Courses broadcast on public television channels can help you review coursework that you're taking in the classroom setting, or they may be your main way of taking a class. Increasingly popular online courses especially give you flexibility about where and when you take your class, as well as opportunities to review course material at your convenience.

> *"Distance education is one of our fastest growing areas of enrollment. We encourage students, especially younger ones, to take a combined program of distance and on-campus courses. We feel that the classroom experience is a valuable one that students shouldn't entirely miss. Many of our distance education courses include some classroom requirement such as an orientation or an in-class exam."*
> —Dr. Charlene Nunley, President, Montgomery College (Maryland)

You'll be able to use distance courses strategically to fill gaps in your course requirements. This is especially helpful when you need to take a course but it isn't offered on campus during the semester, or when a course is "closed out," that is, it has reached the maximum number of students who can enroll.

Roy R. Gordon (Montgomery College, Class of 2005) cites his own experience: "I work full time and have a busy travel schedule, so online courses were a great help when courses I needed weren't offered when I needed to take them. By taking a course offered in the summer, I was able to keep to my plan to graduate and enroll in the University of Maryland on time. I took about five online courses over two years. It's not for everyone. It takes a lot of discipline and you really need good basic computer and Internet skills to do well."

Faculty members enjoy teaching distance education courses and find that students benefit from the experience. Rob Jenkins, who teaches English and is the director of The Writers Institute at Georgia Perimeter College, says, "Community colleges tend to be in the forefront of technology. Faculty members like teaching online courses even though it's a lot of work. A different type of community develops. Sometimes students who normally wouldn't speak up in the classroom aren't afraid to state their opinion online. They also ask the professor questions. Students get a lot out of the exchange and discussion among themselves. A community of learners naturally forms."

Remember—distance education courses aren't for everyone, but they can give you some flexibility in scheduling and help you achieve your goals.

How Challenging Will My Courses Be?

Community colleges may offer a relatively fast way to complete a degree or certificate, but students are often surprised that courses aren't a snap. Community college courses are challenging. Many associate's degree and certificate programs are geared to meet industry and technical standards, so you know they're going to be tough. Employers want to hire people who know their stuff, have critical thinking and problem-solving skills, and who can do the job.

Some occupations, especially in the health fields, require passing a certification or licensing examination before you can be employed. These tests are challenging. Your coursework will be designed to prepare you to pass them.

> *"Many students make the mistake of thinking community college is just an extension of high school. They aren't prepared for the college classroom experience, or for the amount of study time required to do the assignments."*
> —Dr. Constance Saulsbery Beck, retired professor of mathematics, Westchester Community College (New York)

Jeffrey Wright, a full-time faculty member in the Aviation Maintenance Technology program at Cincinnati State Technical and Community College, observes, "Part of our job is to prepare students to pass the Federal Aviation Administration (FAA) Airframe and Power Plant certificate examinations, as well as to fulfill the requirements for an Associate of Applied Science degree. The FAA mandates 1,900 hours of attendance to get this license. Students have to pass a total of nine tests—written, oral, and practical—for the license. You need 168 credit hours to get the degree; it's almost like getting a bachelor's degree. The program and curriculum are challenging, but we're preparing students to work on airplanes and engines worth millions of dollars. They have to know what they're doing."

Not all programs are as intensive as this one, but you'll find that whatever you are studying, community college courses will be both challenging and worthwhile.

WHAT WILL BE DIFFERENT FROM HIGH SCHOOL?

Whether it's been a while since you've been in school or you're coming to community college directly from high school, you'll find there may be some aspects of community college that you didn't expect and that take some adjustment.

Touré Muid, who is studying hotel and restaurant management at Bergen Community College (New Jersey), has these observations: "The level of coursework is completely different than in high school. You're expected to do much more. You're much more responsible for your own learning. In high school, teachers tend to walk you through everything to make sure you understand the material and assignments. In college, there's lots and lots of writing and that can be a shock."

It's Not High School!

✓ You'll take charge of your education and be responsible for learning.

✓ You'll be responsible for your course schedule and how you manage your time, attendance, and progress.

✓ Your professors will not be checking up on you to see if you're getting your assignments, readings, and so on, done.

✓ You'll be responsible for knowing and following what the course requirements and policies are once you've been given the syllabus (course outline).

✓ Excuses that probably didn't work in high school—"I didn't have time," "I didn't understand," "The computer ate my homework"—definitely won't work here.

✓ Step-by-step instructions will often not be given for everything. You'll need to decide how to approach a project, research it, and get it done.

✓ More independent reading and study will be expected.

✓ If you need help, there's plenty available, but you'll be in charge of finding and accessing it.

What Will My Instructors Expect from Me?

Your instructors will basically expect that you'll be ready to learn. Be sure to show up for the first day of class with a notebook and pen, ready to begin. Your instructor will distribute the syllabus, or course outline, and then discuss what will happen during the semester, plus his or her expectations for the class.

The syllabus generally tells you information such as

✓ Course requirements and assignments with due dates

✓ Attendance requirements

✓ A list of books and articles that are required reading

✓ Ways to earn extra credit, if offered

✓ How your grade will be determined

✓ Classroom and college policies on issues such as late submission of work, cheating, and plagiarism (using someone's work without permission or acknowledgment)

✓ The professor's expectations about classroom etiquette, that is, acceptable behavior in the classroom

TIP: If it makes you more comfortable to know as much as possible before walking into class, find a student who has taken a course from your professor before. He or she will be able to pass along some of the professor's likes and dislikes and what the professor's expectations will be.

Your instructor will be responsible for

✓ Being well-prepared to teach each class

✓ Treating students with respect

✓ Providing a classroom atmosphere that encourages learning and respect for a diversity of opinions

✓ Covering the material outlined in the syllabus and upholding the stated policies on assignments, tests, attendance, and other items outlined in the syllabus

✓ Grading you fairly and letting you know your progress in class by returning tests, essays, and other assignments promptly

✓ Providing you with ways to contact him or her for assistance or if a problem arises

✓ Following the college's policies on issues such as discrimination

Each instructor will have his or her own style of teaching. Some will prefer to lecture and will allow you to ask questions. Others will focus on classroom discussion and student participation as a way to present and review material. Some may emphasize individual or team presentations. Others may switch among all these styles during the semester. Whatever the teaching style, it will be up to you to adapt to their styles of presentation to get the most out of class.

As the student, you will be expected to:

✓ Know the instructor's requirements for each class

✓ Attend class

✓ Actively participate in class by asking and answering questions and contributing to discussions

✓ Behave courteously in class

✓ Respect the rights and opinions of others

✓ Complete assignments on time

✓ Monitor your progress in class and get help when you need it

✓ Know your professors' policies about issues such as attendance and make-up exams

How Busy Will I Be?

Now that you have the general overview of what you can expect in class, you can begin to see that being a community college student will require a lot of time and effort on your part.

If you're like most community colleges students, however, going to school will not be your only activity or responsibility. Most students have a part-time or full-time job, family, a social life, and, perhaps, involvement in community activities. You'll be juggling a lot already. Here are some factors you'll need to take into account as you determine what will make community college manageable for you.

To be considered a full-time student, you will usually take at least 12 credits a semester. This probably amounts to three or four courses each semester. If you're taking a three-credit course, that means you'll have three hours of in-class time each week. Multiply that by 4 classes and you've got 12 hours of time you'll be expected to be in class that week. If you take less than 12 credit hours a semester, you will be considered a part-time student, but the class time hours and time required to do assignments still add up. Courses that include labs or "clinicals," such as many courses in the sciences and health professions, end up demanding far more than the stated 6 hours of lab or clinical time per week.

You might spend a full day on campus, take an early morning course and then go to work, or finish your work day and arrive on campus for the evening session. Because community colleges try to be as flexible as possible with scheduling, many of them also offer weekend courses or special programs with weekend sessions.

Of course, in addition to attending class, you will also have to find the time outside of class to study, complete assignments, and write any assigned reports. Both part-time and full-time students tend to underestimate just how much time they'll have to spend on coursework outside of the classroom.

So, no matter how many courses you take or when you take them, attending college requires a substantial investment of time. Add the commute to campus plus your other daily activities and responsibilities, and you'll have quite a busy week.

Although there is no typical day for anyone, here's an example of one part-time student/full-time employee's day.

SNAPSHOT: Musa Saquee is attending college part time and completing some basic skills courses before seeking admission to the radiologic technician program at Gwinnett Technical College (Georgia). Because of financial constraints, he is working nearly full time as a convention service attendant at a nearby hotel. He describes a typical day as: "My day begins at 6 A.M. and ends about 11:30 P.M. I'm out of the house by 6:30 A.M. so I can arrive a few minutes before my 7:30 A.M. English class. I have another class at 1 P.M. and then I'm due at work at 3 P.M. By the time I get home it's 11:30 P.M. or later. I'm often too tired to study then so I try to go to the library between my classes to prepare my assignments. It's hard to find enough time to study when you're working full time. I'm hoping to reduce the number of hours I work and to find a job on campus so I can take more courses and have more time to devote to my studies."

Now that you have some idea of what to expect in the classroom and from your instructors, as well as some of the demands on your time, you'll need to know how you can be successful in your studies, as well as what campus resources will be available to help you. The next chapter will offer advice from students, professors, and administrators about what to do.

Find Out More

✦ *Roadways to Success,* 3rd edition, by James C. Williamson, Debra A. McCandrew, and Charles T. Muse (Upper Saddle River: Pearson Education, Inc., 2004), offers valuable information for community college students about the classroom experience, campus resources, and ways to be successful in achieving your educational and personal goals. www.prenhall.com/williamson has an interactive Web site for self-quizzes outlined in the text.

✦ The Lumina Foundation, a private foundation dedicated to helping all people achieve their potential through education, has information on its Web site (www.luminafoundation.com) for adults returning to college. Click on "Adult Learners." See their *Focus* magazine's *Lifelong Learning* edition, which is available online or by calling 317-951-5300.

Keep on Course: How Can I Be Successful in Community College?

> 66 *To get the most out of your community college experience, you need to understand that you are responsible for your education and learning. Whatever situation presents itself—classes, other students, teachers, extracurricular activities—all these situations are learning experiences, and it's your responsibility to take maximum advantage of them. Otherwise, you're shortchanging yourself.* 99

—Kimberly Newman, Montgomery College (Maryland), Class of 2006

Being in college is as much about learning how to be a student as it is about learning the subject matter. Whether you're coming directly from high school or have been out of school for some time, you'll still have some culture shock and will need some time to adjust and make the transition.

Here are some ways that you'll be able to make the most of your time at community college and be successful.

Realize That You're in Charge!

Community college requires that you take an active role in your education. Although professors are there to teach and college staff is there to help, you're the one who will be responsible for your education and for getting the most from your experience.

College is much more self-directed than high school, where parents and teachers tended to nudge you along in the right direction and monitor your progress. It's the difference between being in the driver's seat and just being a passenger in the car.

If you're a recent high school graduate, you might think "Great, I'm free, and now I can do what I want." That's true, but you're also free to succeed or fail. It's all up to you. Students who take on the responsibility for their education are often the most successful. They're students who

- ✓ Take their studies seriously, make the effort to participate, and do well in class
- ✓ Make contact with other students, professors, and staff at the college
- ✓ Know where and how to get help when they need it
- ✓ Take advantage of the full range of services available
- ✓ Become as active as possible in the life of the college

Set Goals and Priorities for Yourself

If you're just out of high school, you may not know exactly what you want to study or what career path you want to follow. You can, however, set some basic short-term and long-term goals, as well as priorities, for yourself.

Doing so will help you stay focused on what's important to you and will help you succeed in achieving your goals. Even students who know exactly what they want out of community college need to set goals to stay on track.

A short-term goal might be to enroll in a class that looks interesting to you and to do well in it. A longer-term goal might be to take some honors classes. Long-term goals might be to get your degree and find a satisfying career with a job that pays well.

A priority is something that is important at this moment. For example, your priority could be to study rather than go out with friends. Your goals and priorities will probably change as you go through community college.

Amanda Alkins started out thinking she only wanted to complete her AAS degree in nursing at Community College of Philadelphia, get her nurse's license, and start work. She discovered, however, that "the more I learn, the more I realize how much there is to know in my field. Now, I'm sure I'll go on to get my bachelor's degree, even if I work for some time beforehand. I hadn't expected I would want to do that when I started out. I thought 'I just want my AAS degree and to get out.'"

If you're an adult student, even if you have a specific educational objective in mind, you may also find that your goals will change as you progress through your studies.

SNAPSHOT: Aimee Tootsey is a 37-year-old mother of two teenage daughters who returned to school at Montgomery College (Maryland) in 2001 and who graduated in 2005. She says: "I loved history, and thought I would love to be a high school history teacher. My experiences at community college showed me that I could do more with my education than I thought. I could teach high school, go into museum studies, or even get a PhD in history. Whatever path I choose, I hope someday to have the opportunity to assist other adult students to find their paths to educational fulfillment."

Balance Your Personal, Work, and Academic Life

Whether you're a recent high school graduate who is still living at home or a working adult with a family, you'll still be juggling a lot of balls at one time. You'll need time to make some adjustments so that you'll be able to manage everything, especially making enough time for your coursework and assignments.

Constance Saulsbery Beck, retired mathematics professor, Westchester Community College (New York), offers this advice: "Some students try to do way too much on the outside. They're carrying 15 and 16 credits and working a full-time job. They're surprised that they're not doing well.

"You may have to decide to cut back on work or on the number of credits you're taking. You need to be realistic about how much time you can work and actually do well in school. It may be worth spending an extra semester or two to do well rather than to take too many credits and do poorly, especially if you want to transfer. It's a matter of setting of priorities for your work, social, and academic life. Sometimes it just boils down to: 'Do you want a new car or to get your degree more quickly?'"

Your family can help make the balancing act easier. To be supportive, they'll need to understand what you're trying to accomplish.

Delores Smalls, Coordinator of Educational Counseling Services, Nassau Community College (New York), says, "It's important to realize that when you enroll in college, this has an impact on *everyone* in your family. So everyone needs some time to adjust. Even students who are still living at home have responsibilities. Talk to your family about what you're doing at college so they'll understand your schedule and the time you need to spend on your studies. It will make life easier for everyone."

Take Responsibility for Understanding the College's Requirements

Remember, you'll be in charge of your education. You'll be expected to know or find out about rules, regulations, course and major requirements, graduation requirements, financial aid, and so on.

Two invaluable sources of information about your college's requirements, policies, and student code of conduct are the *college or course catalog* (sometimes called a bulletin) and the *student handbook*. Some of their information may overlap, but basically everything you will need to know about attending your community college will be in these two very important publications (available online and in print).

Delores Smalls says, "'I didn't know' isn't an acceptable excuse at college. All the information you need to be successful is available—through student services and other campus offices, as well as online and in print. Almost everything a student needs to know is in your college catalog and your student handbook. Don't put them away. Carry them with you and use them! Read the information in them and absorb it."

Get to Know People

You'll have plenty of opportunity to meet new people—staff, professors, other students. Take some time to get to know them. You never know who might be your biggest inspiration or who might become a lifelong friend.

MAKE A CONNECTION WITH COLLEGE STAFF

Although you may be able to perform many functions online, such as registering for classes, selecting your course schedule, or applying for financial aid, take some time to meet the college staff in various offices, such as financial aid, the career center, student affairs, in person.

You'll find this is helpful before you even get into community college. You'll know where to go for help when you need it. You'll have a personal connection with someone when you run into a problem such as not getting your financial aid submitted on time, or when you don't understand what courses you need to take in your major.

INTRODUCE YOURSELF TO YOUR PROFESSORS

Even in a small classroom, it's easy to be invisible and just be another name on a student list. Remember, professors (also called instructors or faculty members) often teach 5 or more classes a week, so they'll have a total of 100–150 students in their classes.

Get to know your professor's name and office hours (the time a professor will be available in his or her office), and make an appointment to introduce yourself. Professors are often surprised by how few students visit them during office hours for an appointment or for an impromptu visit. Their doors are open; go see them!

You may not have quite as much opportunity to meet an adjunct (part-time) professor. These people are usually respected individuals working in their field, so they have their own careers to attend to when not in the classroom. You can still contact your instructors by email and arrange to meet with them after class.

By getting to know your instructors, you'll be letting them know that you're interested in their courses and are serious about your studies. You'll also feel more comfortable seeking their help if you run into a problem in a course or need a recommendation for the future.

> *"Definitely get to know your professors. It can't hurt. I had a situation where I couldn't get a book for my statistics class because it was sold out. I knew the professor and he helped me get a copy so I wouldn't be left behind when the course started."*
> —Touré Muid, Hotel and Restaurant Management Major, Bergen Community College (New Jersey)

There are many ways to get to know your professors. Delores Smalls not only counsels students, but also teaches a college skills/orientation class for entering students. As an assignment for that class, she requires students to make appointments with instructors, interview them about their careers and what they prefer in the classroom, and how students can improve classroom performance. Students write essays about their experiences and share them in class. Smalls says "By making that connection, students see their instructors in a totally different light, as approachable and willing to help."

You might want to try this method to get to know a professor in a field that interests you when you make a visit to the college campus, when you first enroll, or when you have a new professor.

MAKE A CONNECTION WITH OTHER STUDENTS

Getting to know someone in your class or by participating in a club or other activity on campus has its own rewards (see Chapter 9 for a discussion of campus activities).

✓ You'll see you're not alone because other students share similar problems.

✓ You'll have a network of support and people who can help you if you miss a class and need some notes.

✓ You'll have some fun getting to know someone new whose background and outlook on life might be different from yours.

Victor B. Smith, Sr., a returning adult student who is actively involved in student government and campus activities at Community College of Philadelphia, says, "If, after five weeks in class, you haven't spoken to anyone and tried to connect, you're wasting your time. You're in a place where classes are small. The instructor knows your face and your name. There's an opportunity to meet some truly great people, including your instructor. You need to take it. I'm in a class now with five students whom I met in other courses. We all know each other. It's like a family reunion."

> *"Because classes are small, you have a chance to interact on a personal level with other students. In my speech and reading classes, we all helped each other. Community college is like having a larger family. You can make friends and connections for life."*
>
> Marga C. Fripp, Montgomery College
> (Maryland), Class of 2005

Tips for Academic Success

There are many ways that you can make your classroom experience rewarding and enjoyable, as well as easier. Some of them are simple, such as showing up for class; others might not be obvious to you, especially if you're new to college. By following the tips below, you'll get more out of your studies and time on campus.

BE THERE!

Sure, it will ultimately be up to you whether or not you attend class. You should be aware that many professors consider attendance to be a critical part of the learning process. Whether or not they take attendance, they expect you to show up for class.

Victor B. Smith, Sr. says, "We've all been there. You might think it's more interesting to hang out with your friends or family, or it might be raining and you just don't feel like you want to go. My advice is: Get yourself to class. If you don't, one thing will lead to another. You'll find it's easy to miss a second and third class. You're already behind if you don't make it to class."

There are lots of excellent reasons to attend class.

✓ Good attendance impresses upon your professor that you take your coursework and your responsibilities as a student seriously.

✓ Because classroom lectures, assignment review, and discussions are an important part of the learning process, you have to be there to gain the best possible understanding of the subject matter.

✓ Assignments are reviewed and given out in class. If you miss class, you may miss an assignment or important information about an upcoming quiz or test.

✓ In many cases, professors will take attendance and even consider it as part of your grade!

TIP: Plan ahead. You'll know when you have an appointment or another conflict that might prevent you from coming to class. Tell your professor and work out a way to get your assignments from another student. You'll also need a back-up plan for emergencies! If your babysitter doesn't show up, the car breaks down, or the bus doesn't come, it's still up to you to get to class. Know what you'll do if you run into a problem.

Also, it's not okay just to disappear from class without an explanation. Cathie Seidman, a full-time faculty member at Hudson County Community College (New Jersey), says "For many foreign-born or immigrant students, family is everything, so when a family problem arises, students often don't think about telling their professors that they won't be in class. They just go. When they return, they've got more problems than when they left. Be sure to explain to your professors what's going on so they can help you."

SPEAK UP!

Make a contribution with a question or stimulate discussion about an issue or problem with your classmates. Exchanges of information among students and between the instructor and students are rich sources of learning.

You'll impress your professors with good questions and discussion points. They'll know that you're taking an active interest in the course and that you're a serious student.

You'll also get to know your fellow students by exchanging ideas with them. You'll find you'll enjoy the class more if you actively participate.

KNOW HOW TO WRITE—AS WELL AS TO SPEAK—YOUR PIECE

Sure, there will be multiple-choice, fill-in the blanks, and open-ended questions; the sorts of tests that you're used to taking. But in community college, you'll also be writing a lot. You'll need to know how to develop an argument and support that argument with facts, not just select the right answer from a choice of several. You'll be writing research papers, essays, journals, reports, presentations for class, and many other materials.

The writing requirement is also one reason students are given assessment and placement tests to determine basic reading and writing skills and are not allowed to progress to college-level courses until they are proficient in these areas. (See Chapter 5 for more information about assessment and placement tests.)

You can give yourself a head start by taking a writing course and brushing up on grammar, punctuation, spelling, and vocabulary before you enroll. You'll also be able to improve your writing skills at your college's writing center or other academic resource centers on campus.

In addition to good writing skills, you'll need good oral communications skills. You may be giving in-class presentations and may be working in teams on problems and papers. So a speech class might also be in order.

AVOID AN END-OF-THE-SEMESTER PILEUP!

Expect to have assignments that you need to do every day. Professors understand that it is often difficult to keep up with the pace of class work, but assignments are an essential learning tool.

Each course you take will carry a certain number of *credit hours*. For example, a three-credit course usually means that you will spend three hours a week in class. Multiply that by four classes and you're at a full-time schedule of twelve credit hours.

This may not sound like much, but each class will likely have daily assignments, plus papers to write, quizzes, tests, problems to solve, and so on. You'll need time to review materials outside of class. The amount of work to be done adds up quickly.

TIP: Students frequently underestimate the amount of time that it takes to do assignments and prepare for class. The rule of thumb is that you'll need at least two hours of study time for each hour of class that you're taking.

You'll need to study and do your daily assignments, as well as work on your longer-term tasks throughout the semester. Don't let them pile up until the end of the semester when you'll be pressed for time and have other things to worry about like a final exam.

Many assignments, such as reading or practicing math problems, don't need to be handed in for grading. That doesn't mean you can or should skip over them. They're meant to help you learn the material, so do them whether or not they'll be graded.

Stephen Bassett, instructor of anatomy and physiology and chairperson of the science department at Southeast Community College (Nebraska), says, "You need to do the work for each course. It helps to try to prepare for each class by pretending that you have a test in that class the very next day."

> *"I wasn't prepared for the amount of homework that you have in college here. Every course I'm taking has assignments due each day. Part of it is a difference with the educational system in my home country of Sierra Leone. But some of it is that professors here expect a lot. And they don't want to hear about how you've got a lot of work for another course and that you couldn't do the work for theirs. They want results!"*
> —Musa Saquee, an adult student at Gwinnett Technical College (Georgia)

BE A NEAT FREAK!

Most professors will expect your written assignments to be done on a computer, or, if done by hand, to be neat and easy to read. Written presentations should be well-organized. Be sure to review your work for spelling and grammatical errors. Even if you run the computer spell and grammar check, it doesn't catch everything. It helps sometimes to have someone else review your work for errors.

Follow the professor's instructions for presentation! If the instructions say staple all the pages together, staple them. If a cover sheet is required, put one on! Nothing annoys professors more than getting a document that looks as though you couldn't be bothered to follow their instructions.

If you have poor computer skills or lack access to a computer, you'll want to brush up on these skills before you enroll. Once in college, there will be a study center or academic computing center where you can continue to upgrade your skills. If you don't have a computer, you'll be able to access one there too. Off campus, computers are often available at your local public library.

Be aware that things can go wrong with computers, often at the worst possible time. Don't type for long periods without saving your work, and back up your work on disk frequently. Otherwise, you may be the unlucky one who loses your paper the night before it's due.

> **TIP:** In-class tests may be handwritten, so make sure your handwriting can be read! It's easy to get sloppy when you're used to typing everything on a computer. Don't jeopardize your grade because the professor can't read your answers.

MAKE THE GRADE

Many factors will count in your grade, depending on what your instructors require in each course: attendance, completion of assignments, quizzes, midterm and final examinations, extra credit assignments, and so on.

Not all assignments will carry the same value. For example, your professor might consider a research paper to count for 15 percent of your grade, the midterm to count 25 percent of the grade, completed homework assignments to be 15 percent, attendance to be 10 percent, and the final to be worth 35 percent. Usually the grading scale is as follows (with "+" or "−" next to the letter grade):

90–100 = A

80–89 = B

70–79 = C

60–69 = D

0–59 = F

Unlike high school, where you might be quizzed regularly on classroom material or have a series of mini-projects to boost your grade, some professors may only use a midterm and final examination for grades. So, if you either miss an exam or do poorly, you'll end up with a less-than-desirable grade.

MIND YOUR MANNERS

Manners aren't only for special occasions or for your life outside the classroom. Ask any professor.

"A lot of students in class act like they're watching television. They get up, wander off, get a drink of water or a snack, and come back, expecting to be able to pick up the thread of the class where they left off. It's somewhat understandable given the prominence of television in our society, but it's still distracting to the instructor and the class."

—Dr. Anita Schwartz, Professor of Anthropology, Nassau Community College (New York)

Follow these simple rules and you'll impress your professors by avoiding some of their pet peeves. You'll make your life in class and that of your fellow students more enjoyable.

✓ Know your instructors' names and address them appropriately. They'll tell you at the beginning of class whether they prefer to be called by their first name, or their title—Mister, Miss, Ms., Mrs., Doctor, or Professor.

✓ Be on time. Being late all the time isn't okay. You miss too much class material and disrupt other students' concentration with your late arrival. Don't come late to class and ask, "Did I miss anything?" Of course you did; you weren't there! Professors don't like to repeat themselves and will expect you to get notes about material you missed from a classmate. If you are late, take your seat quietly on the side or in the back. Don't walk directly in front of the professor.

TIP: Sit in the front of the class. You'll be able to pay more attention and your professor will know you're interested.

✓ Don't leave your seat in the middle of class to answer your cell phone, buy a soda or snack, or to go to the bathroom unless it's really necessary.

✓ Don't take a call on your cell phone in class. Turn it off when you get there.

✓ Save your conversation with your classmates for before or after class. Focus on the professor, classroom discussion, and what's being taught.

✓ If you miss an examination and scheduled make-up tests, you'd better have a good reason. Professors don't like to, and sometimes can't, make special test arrangements just for you.

✓ Reserve long or difficult questions for an office appointment with the professor. Hogging the floor during class deprives other students of a chance to ask questions or discuss issues. Make an appointment with the professor to have that discussion. You'll both have more time to talk – it's why professors have office hours.

> **TIP:** It never hurts to say "Thank you" to your professor for a class you've particularly enjoyed or for some special help you've received. You'd be surprised; it makes their day.

HANDS OFF SOMEONE ELSE'S WORK!

With all the information available online, it's tempting to try to get some help with all those papers, or maybe to borrow another student's work. Presenting someone else's work as your own (plagiarism) will be viewed very seriously. It can result not only in getting an "F" but also in other disciplinary action by the college. Plagiarism is against the college rules and is a serious breach of ethics.

Plagiarism includes the intentional or unintentional copying of material from the Internet, books, journals, magazines, or other printed documents. Professors can spot plagiarism almost immediately because it is too polished, too academic, or just doesn't sound like a student. Find out from your instructor how you should cite (acknowledge) others' work in your papers. Ask your instructor or a librarian if you're unsure about whether or not something is plagiarism.

> **TIP:** Foreign-born students should keep in mind that copying a known author's work without proper citation is not acceptable here, although in their own countries it might be a sign of honor and respect for the author.

STUDY! STUDY! STUDY!

Student Touré Muid says the key to success is: "Stay focused! You need to teach yourself self-discipline. It's all up to you. If you procrastinate doing your work, you'll fall behind before you even know it."

Here are some ways to help you get and stay focused.

✓ Set up a study schedule and stick to it.

✓ Create a productive study environment. Set aside a special space dedicated for studying, if you can.

✓ Use time between classes to study and do assignments.

✓ Review your notes after each class.

✓ Give yourself self-tests often. Check out online sources of help including tutoring, tutorials, and reviews connected to your textbook.

✓ Do your assignments as soon as possible. Don't leave your work for several days—you may forget the professor's instructions.

✓ Join a study group for informal support from your fellow students. When setting up a study group, be sure to include students with various levels of understanding and knowledge, including someone who is doing well in class, to get the most out of your study time together. If no one understands the material, you won't be able to help each other.

TIP: Find a study buddy. Roy R. Gordon, a 49-year-old returning adult student (Montgomery College, Maryland), says "My honors program required that we have a study buddy. Mine was an African-American young woman in her late twenties. We came from very different backgrounds so it was fun getting to know each other. We also each had a different learning and studying style. I learn better with a technique called mind mapping. She learned best by flash cards. We taught each other a lot and both did well in the class. Having a study buddy is a good method for any community college student to get the most out of a course."

CHALLENGE YOURSELF WITH HONORS

Students who excel academically may be eligible to apply for or to be invited to participate in an honors program based on their grade point average. More than one-third of all community colleges offer this type of special program.[1]

Depending on your college, these programs range from standard courses with special additional requirements, such as a research paper, for honors students to specially designed honors courses to highly structured programs where students take all their coursework together.[2] Part-time and full-time students who meet the criteria are eligible to participate.

> *"In community college, you have a choice of challenging yourself, or just cruising through your studies trying to take easy courses. My advice would be to challenge yourself to be your best. Taking some honors courses helps you do that."*
> —Judith Martinez, Montgomery College (Maryland), Class of 2004

According to Michael Berkowitz, co-director of the honors program at Westchester Community College (New York), some of the advantages of taking honors courses are:

✓ Often the best and most creative faculty members teach these courses. Depending on the program, you may also have a faculty member as a mentor.

✓ You'll get to study subjects in more depth for a richer learning experience (smaller classes/exciting topics).

✓ You'll build an academic record that will help pave your way into a high-quality four-year institution through a transfer.

✓ You'll have academic, internship, scholarship, and extracurricular opportunities that might not be available to students who aren't in the honors program.

In addition, students in honors programs have their honors courses noted on their transcripts and may earn membership in Phi Theta Kappa, the international honor society of community colleges.

Aimee Tootsey (Montgomery College, Maryland) says, "I was looking for a challenge and wanted more than a four-wall classroom education. In the Millennium Scholars honors program, for part-time and returning adult students, I traveled to England and attended the Cambridge University International Summer School for two weeks, took two British history courses, and got to tour landmarks, buildings, and tombs of people I had only read about. I've had two museum internships at the Smithsonian Institution in Washington, D.C. that were fully funded by the college. In addition, I made the Maryland All-State Academic Team, was inducted into Phi Theta Kappa honor society, and received a merit scholarship to attend the college of my choice, Hood College in Frederick, Maryland, to study history. Being in the honors program and community college has broadened my perspective about what I am capable of achieving. Thanks to the outstanding professors at Montgomery College and the Millenium Scholars honors program, the world has become my classroom."

Know What Resources Are Available to You

Community colleges have terrific resources to help you in just about every way possible: on-campus day centers; academic support centers; special offices for international students, students with disabilities, women students, and adult students; financial aid offices; career centers. The list goes on. It pays to know what's available so you'll be able to seek assistance when you need it.

Marga C. Fripp says, "Community college is a great experience and there are lots of people to help you, but when I decided to enroll no one said: 'Oh, good! Marga is here! Let's see what she needs.' You have to do your own research, get to know the campus, people, and services available, find out what's required and who can help you out. It can take some digging, but you'll find the help you need. Make a personal connection and make yourself visible. You have to be motivated to succeed. It's no one's responsibility but yours."

So college staff will be there to help, but you'll have to do the asking. It will be your responsibility to make sure that you access the services, have all your paperwork in order, fill out and file forms on time, know what your course, major, and graduation requirements are, and do your job in the classroom. *Your progress and success are ultimately your responsibility.*

GET HELP WHEN YOU NEED IT

One of the best things about community college is that you are not alone. Everyone, even students who do well in their studies, needs help occasionally. You've already learned that there will be many people on campus who will help you plan your academic program, think about possible careers, assist you with financial aid, and so on.

Help will also be available if you start having problems in class, or if personal and family issues arise that might affect your academic performance.

> **TIP:** Donald Weigand, Director of Counseling and Student Development, Westchester Community College (New York), says "A major mistake students make is not to get help as soon as they begin to have trouble. Trouble can take many forms—from not understanding assignments to not doing well on a test to having a family crisis."

Students who know about the academic support center, writing lab, tutoring services, and other resources on campus are going to be the ones who get help early and who succeed.

Don't Wait—Take Action!

If you are having a problem, whether it's in class or in your personal life, here are three quick ways to start to get help.

1. Talk to your professor. Your professor is one of your best resources and will be your first line of defense. If you can't see your professor during scheduled office hours, ask if you can call or email him or her.

2. Contact an academic advisor.

3. Go to one of the counseling services, or if you're in a special program, talk to a staff member.

Professors—Your First Lifeline

Your professors will be willing to help you understand the classroom materials and assignments, but you'll have to ask for their assistance.

Sometimes, your problem will be that you simply do not understand what you've been asked to do. Your professor, not other students, will be the best source of information on all topics related to the course.

> **TIP:** Don't be afraid to ask for help. Professors don't bite! But ask early. The day before a big test isn't the time to knock on your professor's door and ask him or her to review materials with you. Also have a specific question in mind. Don't just say "I don't understand." Instead, say "I have a question about the reading material you assigned" or "about this particular algebra problem."

Professors aren't interested in excuses (and they do know them all), but they will listen and help with real problems. They know that you're juggling lots of responsibilities and that there will be times that you need some flexibility and help.

If a problem arises, you'll need to let your professors know. They can't help you work out a solution unless they know that you've got a problem.

Rob Jenkins, associate professor of English, and director of The Writers Institute, who also served as academic dean at Georgia Perimeter College, says, "Our students often have tough lives. I've even had students call me from jail to say they'll be missing an exam and ask when they can do the make-up. The fact that they persevere despite their problems is a testimony to the human spirit. As their professor, you might not be the right person to help them solve their problem, but you can help them find someone on campus who can. Sometimes, they just need someone to listen to them."

You don't have to confide more than you wish to your professor; simply explain the obstacles you are facing and see what can be done to help you.

SNAPSHOT: Todd Sullivan (Copiah-Lincoln Community College, Mississippi, Class of 2005) found out how valuable personal contact is when he developed skin cancer the second semester of his freshman year. "I had a one-on-one relationship with my professors. They knew me and knew I was serious about my studies. During my year of chemotherapy, my professors worked with me to make sure I could keep up with classes and assignments. Having their help plus that of my friends, club advisors, and family gave me the support network I needed to get through it. Now I'm in a pre-med program at the University of Mississippi and on my way to becoming a doctor."

Advisors—On Duty All Year Round

When you first register for community college you'll meet an academic advisor, who will help you select classes. Later on, when you choose a major, a faculty advisor in your department will be available to assist you. Even if you are not required to consult with an academic advisor, it's a good idea to get to know an advisor personally. They will help you troubleshoot and avoid a lot of problems.

Advisors will be available throughout the year to help you with academic problems and choices. They can help you answer questions such as: "I'm not doing well in this course. What should I do? Should I continue or should I drop it? Is it too late to withdraw from class? What courses do I still need to graduate? I just got a letter saying I'm on academic probation. What does that mean? What courses do I need to satisfy the requirements in my major? What are the requirements to get a degree or certificate in this field?"

Keep in touch with them during the year and see them *before* you get into trouble. Much as they like to help, advisors don't come searching for you. You'll be responsible for getting the help you need.

Danger Points During the Semester!

Dr. Marvin Bright, Dean of Students, Community College of Philadelphia says there are three main times during a semester (15–16 weeks) when students tend to find themselves in trouble and at a decision-making point about continuing with a class.

1. "The first is at two to four weeks, when students are new to a course and maybe nothing seems to be going right—they don't understand the course outline or expectations, they haven't been able to get their books, or they haven't connected with the professor or other students.

2. "The second is when they're a third on halfway through the course. The student and professor will know if the student is in trouble by quiz grades, the midterm grade, the class attendance record and participation, and other factors.

3. "The third point is week 8 or 9 when there's still a possibility to withdraw rather than wind up with a failing grade. Neither option is really desirable because they both go on your record and they can affect your financial aid eligibility. By this time, it's often too late to get help, and you're stuck with not-very-attractive choices."

Counseling Centers

As noted above and elsewhere, you'll have as much help as you want with academic, career, and financial aid issues. Sometimes, however, you may need help with other issues at a personal or family level.

Personal and family issues especially can take a hidden toll on you when you are in community college. Before you know it, you're not focusing in class, you're missing a few sessions, and you're skipping assignments. Remember that your success at community college is important to your family, too.

> *"Going to see a counselor doesn't mean that you've done something wrong. It means you need some help and we want to give it to you. This isn't like high school where, frequently, when you're sent to the guidance counselor, it's because you're in trouble. Counseling services on campus are there to support and assist you."*
>
> —Donald Weigand, Director of Counseling and Student Development, Westchester Community College (New York)

Counselors will be available to talk out issues, help you sort out options, and help you decide on a course of action that can help you stay focused and in school even though other aspects of your life are unsettled.

Programs will also be available to help you deal with medical and health problems, as well as serious issues such as alcohol and drug abuse problems.

Counseling sessions are confidential, so you don't have to worry that your problems will become public. Your professor can be sympathetic and help to a certain extent, but you might need some additional professional assistance to help you resolve your issues. It's available, so take advantage of it.

Your college may have a separate center or several centers that can help you with these issues. You'll want to check with your office of student affairs or student services to see what services are available on your campus. In addition, should you need more assistance than the college can offer, counselors will be able to direct you to external resources and professionals who can help you.

OTHER CAMPUS RESOURCES FOR ACADEMIC SUCCESS

Community college is really geared to helping you succeed at every level. Be sure to take advantage of additional academic resources on campus and online to help you do as well as you possibly can do in your coursework. It's challenging, but help is available.

Academic Support

Most colleges have a center or several specialized centers dedicated to offering you additional academic support in a broad range of subjects, especially in basic skills such as reading, writing, and mathematics. These academic support centers or learning resource centers offer a variety of types of assistance ranging from individual or group tutoring to access to computer-based or online course reviews. They may also be specialized, such as a writing center, a mathematics center, or an academic computer center to help you sharpen your basic computer skills.

At Westchester Community College in New York, for example, the Academic Support Center operates on a walk-in basis. As Joanna Peters, a lab coordinator, points out, "This system allows students to seek help easily when they need it. Our tutors know how to pinpoint their needs and address their problems. We find that students start to view the Academic Support Center as a safe haven and a comfortable place to be, especially once they develop a rapport with the tutors.

"The Center is a place where students can also connect with other students. They even start to help each other. Our biggest issue is that students who need help often do not come to the Center for assistance or they come too late in the semester. But when they do, we give them highly personal attention."

> *"The Academic Support Center isn't just for students who are underprepared in English, mathematics, or reading. It's also for the student who has a B+ grade and wants an A. We also help students learn how to organize themselves into the role of student, as much as we help them develop their academic skills."*
>
> —Joanna Peters, Lab Coordinator, Westchester Community College (New York)

You'll want to see what academic support services are available at the departmental level also. For example, if you're studying computer science or physics, your department may offer tutoring services because these are difficult subjects that require special knowledge. Tutoring is usually available free of charge, so why not get help when you need it?

College Survival or Skills Courses

Almost every college has a skills course to help you learn to be a good or better student. Sometimes, these courses are recommended for entering students and sometimes they are an actual requirement (often called Freshman Orientation). They are often available during the year as "refresher" courses when you need help.

> **TIP:** Many community colleges have special orientation courses or sessions for adult students (usually 25 years and older) as part of an office of adult student services.

You'll learn good study habits, understand your learning style, improve your note-taking and test-taking skills, learn ways to manage your time and stress—just about anything that is going to help you succeed in your classes.

In addition, many of these courses help you review requirements for your major and understand program requirements. They will get you started right and keep you on the right pathway.

If you weren't a great student in high school or feel you need to brush up on how to be a student, these courses will be well worth the time you put into them. After all, the goal is to succeed, right?

TIP: Many colleges have terrific online resources for student success—time management, study skills, test-taking tips, information about learning styles, memory development, stress management, and other general tips.

The Library

Don't overlook the campus library as a place where you can receive assistance, from finding reference materials to computer access to online courses and email.

Once again, you won't be on your own. Librarians are there to help you access the information you need to do your research papers, find reference materials, and steer you to the right resources for your class work. They're the experts and know where the materials are, so let them be your guides.

You'll find all the materials you'll need including books, magazines, videotapes, CD-ROM databases for research, special materials that your professors have reserved—just about anything you need for your coursework.

Libraries are also centers where computer or study skills are often taught. They can also be your retreat when you need a quiet place to study between classes.

Special Services Offices

Community colleges have many services for students with special needs, such as

- ✓ Students with disabilities
- ✓ Returning adult students
- ✓ Students who are economically disadvantaged
- ✓ Students who are academically at risk
- ✓ Students with limited English proficiency
- ✓ Single parents
- ✓ Women students, including displaced homemakers and wel-fare-to-work program participants
- ✓ International students

You'll find a supportive network of professionals who are famil-iar with your special needs and challenges. Services often include development of an educational plan; free individual and group tutoring; workshops on study skills, test taking, and time man-agement; personal career and academic counseling; and referrals to other departments or community agencies.

Although services are similar to those offered in other college offices, such as counseling, these programs often have separate funding, and focus on the particular needs of these students in making the transition to college, the special issues they face in staying in school, and offer programs targeted to their needs. If you think you'll be eligible for services from one of these special offices, speak with a counselor in that office.

A Special Note about Support Services for Disabled Students

Students with disabilities can receive an outstanding array of aca-demic and other support services at community college, as noted in Chapter 5.

In the classroom, for example, students can have note takers, readers, and sign language interpreters. You might need a device that makes hearing the lecture or classroom discussion easier or a reading machine to assist you. Specially trained tutors can also help you with your homework assignments and with learning the material presented in class. Other types of classroom accommodations can also be made.

It's up to students with disabilities to make the college aware that you qualify for services and to offer documentation of your disability. The college legally cannot contact you about your needs. You must request support services. You may need to register first with your college's office of services for students with disabilities, which will then be able to help you arrange for services.

Find Out More

✦ *The Community College Experience PLUS* by Amy Baldwin (Pearson/Prentice Hall 2007) is an excellent book that gives information about community college culture, transition issues, ways to manage time and stress, and invaluable advice on how to achieve success in the classroom and beyond. See the companion Web site at www.prenhall.com/baldwin for interactive tools.

✦ For adults returning to college, try Mike Doolin's *A Guerrilla Manual for the Adult College Student: How To Go to College (Almost) Full Time in Your Spare Time ... and Still Have Time to Hold Down a Job, Raise a Family, Pay the Bills, and Have Some Fun!* (booklocker.com 2003).

✦ *How to Flunk Out of a Community College: 101 Surefire Strategies That Guarantee Failure* by Cari B. Cannon (Kendall/Hunt Publishing Company, 2005) offers an amusing look at how community college students (or any college student for that matter) can and do sabotage their careers as students. Great advice so you won't do the same!

Keep Engaged: What Else Is There to Do on Campus and Beyond?

> *You get out of community college what you put in. If you let the campus work for you and you work for the campus by being involved, you'll get a lot back in return. My experiences at community college–participating in student clubs and serving as the Vice President of Service for the Phi Theta Kappa honor society–have given me more than I can ever give back.*

—Todd Sullivan, Copiah-Lincoln Community College (Mississippi), Class of 2005.

Community college offers you opportunities to expand your mind and horizons through a variety of on-campus and off-campus activities and learning experiences. By getting involved on campus, exploring the world of work, serving the community, or even seeing what other societies and cultures are like by studying overseas, you'll enrich your classroom experience and help pave the way to your future career or the next step in your education.

What Types of On-Campus Activities Are Offered?

What else is there to do on campus? Plenty! If you can juggle your busy schedule, there are many on-campus activities that will give you a break from studying, help you connect with other students, be a learning experience outside the classroom, and help you build your resumé.

Your studies come first, of course, but experts recommend that you try to find at least one *extracurricular* [beyond coursework] activity that you enjoy. It could be an occasional event, such as going to a play on campus, or a longer-term commitment to a club activity or sport.

Available activities at community colleges can range from drama clubs for budding actors to student government for future community leaders; from student newspapers and television stations for writers and technicians in training to men's and women's *intramural* (within the college) and *intercollegiate* (competitions with teams from other colleges) sports, such as basketball, baseball, football, or soccer.

Student clubs include clubs focused on career interests such as accounting or nursing, clubs organized by students from a particular ethnic or cultural group, arts groups, and community service clubs that focus on projects such as tutoring at-risk children or organizing a food drive, to name a few.

Check with your office of student life or student affairs to see what is available at your campus. At the beginning of each semester or quarter, there will likely be an activities fair on campus where you will be able to find out about extracurricular opportunities. Bulletin boards, college-wide emails, and online postings of events also keep everyone on campus up to date about what's going on.

Judith Martinez (Montgomery College, Maryland, Class of 2004) says, "If you can, definitely take part in extracurricular activities. It adds a lot to your college experience and can give you some great future connections. As president of the Student Ambassadors' Club, an extension of the alumni association, we did campus tours and helped raise money for the college. By representing the student body at alumni events, I met many of the college's graduates. I also played volleyball on the women's club team here just to relieve stress and stay sane. Athletic activities are a great way for students who are excellent athletes, but who weren't recruited by major colleges to continue playing and maybe get that second shot at playing for a four-year school."

WHY SHOULD YOU PARTICIPATE?

Participating in activities beyond the classroom is not only fun, it will also be a way to help you move toward your educational and career goals.

✓ Extracurricular activities count when you apply for many scholarships or are invited to join honor societies.

✓ Employers want well-rounded employees. Participating in extracurricular activities can be a way to gain leadership skills that will serve you well on the job.

✓ Engaged students who integrate themselves into the life of the college tend to be more successful in reaching their goals.

✓ Campus-based activities are also a great way to connect with other students and to gain visibility and recognition on and off campus. Recognition can pave the way to future rewards.

✓ You'll be able to have some fun and relieve stress while learning some new skills.

SNAPSHOT: Victor B. Smith, Sr., a retired state corrections officer and returning adult student at Community College of Philadelphia, says, "I didn't come in expecting anything, just to get my degree and get out. I found out, however, that getting involved gets you noticed and getting noticed leads to unexpected opportunities. I volunteered for the Colonial Admissions team to take high school students on campus tours and help students out during registration. From there, I ran for Student Government president and got elected. I'm also president of the Student Alliance for Policy Issues that's addressing social problems at the college, city, state and national level. I've been invited to be a speaker at student orientation, have been nominated for the National Dean's List, been offered a full scholarship at a local university, expect to be nominated to Phi Theta Kappa, and will graduate next year with the highest honors. You give and you receive. This past year has been one of the best of my life."

Don't forget that community colleges are there for the community also. Many have interesting lecture series, movies, concerts, art exhibitions, special programs for children, international festivals, programs for senior citizens, sports, and many other events and activities that the entire community can enjoy.

They're perfect places to bring your family for a fun or educational event. So, even if you don't have time to join in an organized activity, you can still enjoy spending time on campus outside the classroom.

HONORS SOCIETIES

You'll have an opportunity to shine not only in an honors program or courses, but also to earn membership in an honor society. Honor societies are organizations that recognize academic excellence, and it is indeed an honor to be invited to join one!

The oldest and largest honors society for community college students is Phi Theta Kappa, established in 1918. Phi Theta Kappa emphasizes not only academic achievement, but also engagement in leadership, service, and fellowship through its honors programs. It offers members many opportunities for individual growth and development through its innovative programs.

Both full-time and part-time students, and international students are eligible for membership. You must have completed a minimum of 12 hours of associate degree coursework and have earned a grade point average of 3.5 or higher. You must also maintain your academic standing, usually a 3.25 GPA, throughout your enrollment to remain a member.

FAST FACT: Phi Theta Kappa, the international honor society of two-year colleges, is the largest honor society in the United States, with over 2 million members. It has 1,200 chapters across all 50 states, U.S. territories, Canada, and Germany. See the Phi Theta Kappa Web site, www.ptk.org.

As a member, you'll receive a Gold Key membership pin, and have the chance to

✓ Be eligible for a substantial transfer scholarship to one of over 600 four-year institutions that offer over $36 million in scholarship funds exclusively to Phi Theta Kappa members.

✓ Wear the Phi Theta Kappa gold stole and tassel at graduation.

✓ Participate in special honors study seminars and courses developed at the national level.

✓ Participate in national-level service projects to help combat cancer, promote mental health, and improve literacy.

✓ Attend regional, national, and international leadership conferences and conventions.

✓ Compete for the All-USA Academic Team for community and junior colleges, sponsored by Phi Theta Kappa, *USA Today*, and the American Association of Community Colleges, as well as for your state's Academic Team. Each team opens many doors to additional scholarship opportunities and recognition.

FAST FACT: A new Phi Theta Kappa program, "Leaders of Promise," now offers thirty $1,000 scholarships to community college students who are currently enrolled in school to help them complete their associate's degrees.

Rod Risley, executive director of Phi Theta Kappa says, "Not every Phi Theta Kappa member may have time to participate in the many programs we offer. However, students who engage in our programs and services will be better equipped to compete in the job market or at a senior (four-year) institution. Corporate recruiters aren't just looking for good grades; they're looking for students who are actively engaged in activities. They want students with excellent communication and social skills, leadership abilities, and people who know how to work well together in teams. Universities also want new students who can contribute to the life of the university. Participating in Phi Theta Kappa gives students a competitive edge that they won't get by simply going to class and going home."

SNAPSHOT: "As part of Phi Theta Kappa's international service project on cancer, our chapter focused on the dangers of tanning beds, especially for young people under the age of 18. We gave out sunscreen at campus events, worked on passing a state law requiring parental consent for youth under 18 to use a tanning bed, and started a project with third graders to teach them about caring for their skin. It was very rewarding to lead the chapter as Vice President of Service at this time, especially as I had suffered from skin cancer myself." Todd Sullivan (Copiah-Lincoln Community College, Mississippi, Class of 2005)

You'll also want to check out other honor societies that are associated with your major or career field. For example, the business national honor society is Phi Beta Lambda; it has local chapters at community colleges. *All* honors societies offer benefits and opportunities that will help you move forward, whether you're going directly to work or transferring to a four-year institution.

Connecting Beyond the College Campus

Your community college experience doesn't need to be limited to your campus. There are a variety of programs that can extend your academic experience beyond the classroom. You'll be able to earn credit in the community through work-study experiences (such as internships) and cooperative-education experiences, service-learning experiences, and even study-abroad programs.

INTERNSHIPS

Many businesses, not-for-profit agencies, and educational institutions offer internships for interested students. An internship is a supervised position that will give you on-the-job training and experience in a particular field, while allowing you to earn course credit for the internship. As an intern, you have an assigned mentor at work and usually a faculty member who supervises your internship to make sure you're doing meaningful work.

SNAPSHOT: Igor Levine (Montgomery College, Maryland, Class of 2005) is interested in setting up a global company some day and served as an intern in a commercial real estate company while studying at Montgomery's Macklin Business Institute. He says, "I learned a lot about how to structure a business and about how to be organized and precise about accounting procedures. I also learned how to communicate with business owners. Even if you are going to school full time, you should take advantage of internships. They give you skills and help you learn about what you want to do in life; plus you're building your resumé."

Most internships are unpaid, but don't pass up the opportunity for lack of payment. You'll be working toward your goal of getting a degree, plus internships are great ways to

- ✓ Test drive not only a job, but also the type of work environment in which you'd like to be.
- ✓ Get to know and understand job opportunities available in your field.
- ✓ Learn about your potential career from the inside out. You'll see exactly what it means to be a computer technician, a set designer in a theater, or an accountant in a business.
- ✓ Develop a network of connections that will be helpful for job references and possible future employment.

COOPERATIVE-EDUCATION PROGRAMS

"Learn and earn" best summarizes this type of work-study program, often referred to as "co-op." You'll get credit toward your coursework at the same time that you are earning money working at a job related to your field of study. Sounds like a good deal? It is.

Many vocational and technical programs require that you get hands-on job experience as part of your requirements. That makes sense, doesn't it? How can you be a good electrician or aviation mechanic if you've never worked on a wiring problem or repaired an airplane engine?

Travis Huelsebusch, while a student in the aviation maintenance technology program at Cincinnati State Technical and Community College, worked as a maintenance assistant at a local airport for his mandatory cooperative-education experience. "I needed four credit hours of co-op experience to graduate," says Travis. "The aviation maintenance technology program has contacts with many firms, like DHL and Executive Jet, and airports in the area. They help you identify jobs and set up interviews. If you work full time (30–39 hours) you could earn two credits instead of one credit, plus you're earning some decent money. Co-op is a great way to get practical experience you need, especially in a technical field, while you're still in school. You're not going to get hired unless you know what you're doing. You're going to be expected to perform once you get on the job."

Some colleges help place you in a cooperative-education experience. Others expect you to find a position yourself, although they usually have a listing of available positions at local companies. Depending on your program, you may work while you attend classes, or you might alternate semesters working and studying.

Touré Muid, a hotel and restaurant management major at Bergen Community College (New Jersey), worked in a restaurant for his co-op experience. "I got a realistic picture of what it takes to run a restaurant and of how complicated it is. You need to know a lot more than I thought, ranging from how to run a kitchen and the proper way to prepare food to how to manage employees and figure out wages. I earned two credits for the course plus I also got paid. Now I have work experience I can put on my resumé. It will help when I transfer to a school like Johnson & Wales to get my bachelor's degree and when I look for a job."

Cooperative-education jobs are great ways to enter the workforce in your field and set up a pathway to future employment. They help you

✓ Learn while getting on-the-job training and experience.

✓ Develop a track record of work to build your resume.

✓ Earn money you can use for college and living expenses.

✓ Get to know companies and vice versa.

TIP FOR WORKING STUDENTS: If you are in a program with required cooperative-education experience, you're usually not expected to give up your full-time job. Sometimes, a more advanced course can be substituted for the cooperative-education experience, or, if you're already working in the field, your current work experience may count. Be sure to check out alternatives with your instructors.

SERVICE-LEARNING PROGRAMS

Service learning is an educational experience that links what you learn in the classroom to your work as a volunteer helping to address real needs in your community.

Its goals are for you to learn by putting ideas into action, gain work-related skills, and to become an informed and productive citizen. You'll be applying what you learn in class to issues faced by your community, such as literacy, poverty, or environmental issues.

FAST FACT: A national survey by the American Association of Community Colleges showed that 71 percent of the colleges that responded (271) offered service learning opportunities for students.[1]

According to Nicholas Holton, instructor of mathematics and service learning coordinator at Kirtland Community College (Michigan), "Almost any type of class can have a service-learning component. In our automotive technology course, students repair cars for people who can't afford to do so. Students write about the the automotive skills they applied, reflect on the social and economic reasons that prevented the person from repairing the car, and explain their personal feelings about helping someone in the community.

"One of our students designed her own project that inventoried all of the substandard housing in the county using a model developed by Habitat for Humanity International. She produced a video and CD on the problem. A business student could do a financial audit for a church or not-for-profit agency. A student interested in the environment can help a state park map out its nature trails. There are all types of possibilities."

You can take courses that include service learning as a component, or—at some colleges—take it as an independent module with faculty supervision. Either way, you earn course credit, perform a specified amount of service work (it could be a one-time event or work spread over the semester or longer), do regular assignments, plus write a reflective essay about your experience as part of the course requirements.

You will have a broad range of educational, government, social service, or environmental community partners who cooperate with your college to offer service-learning opportunities.

You may have concerns that you'll be so busy with your studies and work that you won't be able to find the time to do work in the community. Nicholas Holton says, "I always ask my students: 'Would you spend four hours working on a research paper or assignment for a course if it were required?' They always say 'Yes.' Then, I ask them, 'Why not spend that time working outside to help someone and learn about issues affecting your community?' Remember, you're still earning course credit; you're just extending your learning situation beyond the classroom."

Service learning has the following benefits for you, your community, and your college:

✓ You'll be learning by doing and seeing how what you know applies to real-life situations and issues.

✓ You get to feel good about doing something positive for your community, its people, or the environment.

✓ You'll be adding an attractive credential to your resumé for your next educational step or for employment.

✓ Your community gets some help with real issues, and your college gets some good publicity.

STUDY-ABROAD PROGRAMS

Interested in spending three weeks in China learning about its culture? Working and studying in London for several weeks or a semester?

Yes, it's possible at many community colleges as part of their international education efforts to prepare students to be citizens of the world. Since 1967, a growing number of community colleges have had a global outreach through study-abroad programs. You can expand your understanding of other societies and cultures, not only by meeting international students on campus, but through opportunities to spend several weeks, a semester, or even an academic year studying overseas for credit. Although this type of study is an additional expense, scholarships are often available to help you with the costs.

Peg Mauzy, an assistant professor at The Center for Teaching and Learning, directs the London Work/Study Abroad Experience at Frederick Community College (Maryland). She says, "You can't imagine what a great experience this is for students. They come back so changed, so mature, more knowledgeable about what they want to do with their lives. They learn to problem solve, understand what is happening elsewhere in the world, and expand their horizons. It's a metamorphosis for the students."

An overseas study or work experience will help you

✓ Stand out in the crowd on an application to a four-year college.

✓ Improve your marketability and expand your own horizons.

✓ Gain a new perspective on what you want to do in life. Returning students have gone on to study international education and international business, for example, when that wasn't on their initial career agenda at all.

✓ Get a global perspective that will help you in your job and life.

✓ Gain confidence in your ability to solve problems and get along with others.

SNAPSHOT: Peg Mauzy says, "Our program is unusual because it is one semester (15 weeks) long and students are required to work while they're in London. We handle work permits, but they have to be creative and find their own jobs. Working is the immersion point in the program. Students are quite creative about finding jobs. Two students who wanted to work in office jobs saw a well-dressed gentleman on the underground and started talking to him. They both ended up with a job in a bank. Others work in pubs, local colleges or universities, in the theatre, at law firms—anywhere they can find a job. They have the chance to meet and work with people from all over the world because London is so cosmopolitan.

"Students also take three courses taught by American and British professors and earn twelve credit hours for the semester— six for coursework and six for the work experience (two courses are taken online). They live together in dorms with other college students so they have the dorm experience, but abroad. The last two weeks of the program, students are free to travel anywhere they want to go in the U.K. or on the Continent. They must research and plan this part of the trip themselves and explain why they want to go to the places selected. When students return, we have a day on campus when each presents a portfolio of his or her work and educational experiences to the college president and faculty."

Mauzy's advice to students interested in a study-abroad program is

✓ Do some research online to find a program that suits your needs. Many community colleges offer their own programs or work through organizations such as the College Consortium for International Studies.

✓ Don't dismiss the idea of going because of money. Financial aid is available from a variety of sources including your college, local organizations, and special scholarships for overseas study. Even some federal and state financial aid can be applied to the costs of these programs because you'll be earning course credit for the experience.

✓ Parents of younger students should talk to parents whose students have already participated in study-abroad programs.

✓ If there is an information session on campus about study-abroad programs, attend it, as many of your concerns and questions will be answered.

SNAPSHOT: Anna Magdalena Hess graduated with an Associate in Applied Sciences degree in Textile Surface Design from the Fashion Institute of Technology in New York City. While studying at FIT, Anna was selected to participate in a six-week summer study course to study fabric styling at the center of the design world—Florence, Italy. This is a routine summer-abroad program offered by FIT to a small number of students selected on a competitive basis. "I visited many well-known textile mills (like Kretzia) and design studios, and I attended lectures at the Polimoda Art School that is affiliated with the University of Florence and FIT. We went to markets to learn design research methods, and I gained firsthand experience about what it would be like to be a fabric stylist. I prepared a fabric style book based on the art and colors of Italy for presentation at the end of the project and received course credit. It was a terrific experience."

Find Out More

+ Phi Theta Kappa, www.ptk.org, outlines how you earn membership, its special leadership and service programs, and scholarships for transfer students—plus provides links to other scholarship opportunities.

+ Check out the "Learn and Serve America" program of the Corporation for National and Community Service, an independent government agency dedicated to service learning, at www.learnandserve.gov.

+ Find out more about international study-abroad opportunities through your college, which may have a special Office of International Education. The College Consortium for International Studies, www.ccisabroad.org, is a good source of information about accredited college study-abroad programs.

10

Keep Your Future in Sight: What's Next after Community College?

> *One thing no one can ever take away from you is your education. Once you've got it, it's yours. What you make of it is up to you. My advice is: 'Go for it. Don't be afraid to let your light shine. You won't ever be sorry.'*
>
> —Victor B. Smith, Sr.,
> Community College of Philadelphia, Class of 2006

By now, you know community college can open many doors for you and can be one solid rung up on your personal ladder of success.

The path you choose at the beginning of your studies—whether focused on courses in continuing education and/or workforce development, or leading directly to employment or to a transfer to a four-year institution—can enable you to reach the goals you've set for yourself.

One of the best features of a community college is that, no matter which path you travel initially, you will always be able to come home again. Community college will continue to offer you educational, career, social, and cultural opportunities throughout your lifetime.

In this chapter, you'll learn about what assistance will be available for your transition from college to jobs and careers or for your potential transfer to a four-year institution. You'll also learn about the benefits of maintaining contact with your community college.

Employers Will Want You!

You'll be in the right place if you're ready for a job because community colleges work hand in hand with employers to develop and train the workforce.

Community colleges stay on top of current and future employment opportunities through long-term partnerships with businesses, hospitals, not-for-profit organizations, labor unions, chambers of commerce, local educational systems, local, state, and federal government offices, and many others interested in the economic health and well-being of the geographical areas in which they are located.

Additionally, potential employers often participate in community college business advisory councils, and help to develop the curricula offered at community colleges so that the programs offered meet their specific workforce needs. Consequently, these employers know the value of your degree and are poised to give you an opportunity once you've completed whatever training you've undertaken. So, depending on your course of study, there will most likely be a job with your name on it when you finish. As

> *"Our two-year nursing students at Mt. Hood consistently scored higher on their licensing examinations than students in nursing programs at the local four-year colleges. They all had jobs as soon as they graduated and employers who knew the quality of the program competed fiercely over hiring them."*
>
> —Joan Oliver, a retired instructor in nursing, with over 20 years of experience teaching at Mount Hood Community College, Oregon, and Portland Community College, Oregon

a result of your training, you may be able to upgrade your current job or find a new one that matches your newly acquired skills.

Remember that community colleges are not only training you for local or regional employment opportunities. They are also geared to national employment needs and—more and more—to the global marketplace. Your start at your local community college can turn into employment horizons as expansive as you want them to be.

Community colleges are also often one of the major employers in your area, so don't overlook job opportunities right at the campus! If you find you like the welcoming atmosphere of community college as a student, you might also find it an attractive place to work.

USE YOUR CAREER CENTER

Some of the best resources available to prepare you for and to help you find a job are right at your community college: the career center and workforce development office. Counselors in these offices know the job market and employment opportunities in your community (and beyond). Even if you're in one of the "hot" fields with very high demand, such as homeland security or nursing, you still need some help and guidance locating the best job for you.

Take advantage of as many of your career center's services as possible, both early in your college career to identify your career goals, values, and skills, and later when you're nearing the completion of your studies. This is the perfect place to start your job search with personal counseling and online assistance.

Your career center can help you with information about

✓ Effective resume writing

✓ Interview preparation and practice

✓ Job search strategies

✓ Salary information and negotiation skills

✓ Career fair days

✓ Online access to job opportunities

✓ Written and online employment resources and materials

NETWORK, NETWORK, NETWORK!

If you start networking early while you're taking courses, you'll have a full range of people to assist you when you're ready to enter the job market.

Join Organizations

Linda V. Siegmann, a 2005 Tulsa Community College graduate in accounting (now at Tulsa University), advises that joining a student organization—whether it's a professional organization, an honor society, or a service group—is one of the best ways to start making connections for future jobs early in your educational career. "It's easier for employers to connect with a group at a college than with one student. Once you meet someone on campus, you can follow up with them individually. Through contacts I've made on campus, several people from the American Indian Chamber of Commerce and professional accounting organizations where I've been a student member or liaison since community college have been watching my educational career. Some of them have already expressed an interest in hiring me."

Contact Your Instructors

Don't overlook your instructors as potential job leads, even while you're studying! Instructors, especially in vocational and technical programs, are often working in business and industry themselves while they teach, and can be valuable sources of referral.

Frederick A. Howell, Program Director, Computer Publishing/Printing Management, at the Homer S. Gudelsky Institute for Technical Education at Montgomery College, says "If employers need to hire someone, they know they can call me directly and I will refer a student or students to them. Because our program was founded by and is attuned to the needs of the local print industry, we know the market and businesses well and can ensure a good match with a student who has the right set of skills for the job."

Explore Other Networks

As previously discussed in this book, cooperative education placements and internships provide you with a built-in network of companies and individuals who can help you obtain a full-time job when you're ready. You'll also be able to network with graduates of your college. Contact the alumni office at your college and ask if it has a career mentor program or alumni who are willing to give informational interviews about jobs. Your status as a community college student or graduate will be an immediate connection with them.

FAST FACT: Career One-Stop, the National Toll-Free Helpline (877-USA-JOBS) and local One-Stop Career Centers in each state, provide a wide range of workforce assistance and resources. Your community college might even be a One-Stop site. To locate a One-Stop Career Center near you, visit www.careeronestop.org.

Four-Year Colleges Will Want You!

As discussed in previous chapters, community college can be a stepping stone to further education at a four-year institution. Four-year colleges understand that community colleges produce students who will be valuable additions to their campuses. In fact, studies have shown that community college graduates who transfer to four-year colleges and universities perform academically as well as students who have been directly admitted to those institutions[1].

Aim as high as you like when you start thinking about transferring to a four-year institution. Community college transfer students can be found at many private and public colleges and universities across the nation, including highly selective ones such as Smith College, the University of Michigan, and Columbia University, among others. Many state universities and college systems favor qualified students who transfer from a community college in their state and make it easier for them to enroll and gain credit for their community college coursework.

Because you and you alone are ultimately responsible for ensuring your credits get transferred, you'll need to understand the transfer process and requirements. Your community college transfer office, as well as the transfer office of the four-year institution where you intend to apply, will be your best sources of information. You'll also need to get an early start, and the transfer timeline later in this chapter will be helpful to your planning process.

SNAPSHOT: Pamela Karwasinski was 40 when she was admitted to prestigious Smith College after graduating from Atlantic County (now Cape) Community College (New Jersey). Married and a mother at an early age, Pamela grew up in a rural area of New Jersey in an economically depressed family under difficult circumstances. In her twenties she returned to school for her GED. After she separated from her husband, she realized she needed more education. Through the help of a local community college guidance counselor she enrolled in the college's displaced homemakers program, which she attended for a year before moving and enrolling in ACCC.

"I wasn't convinced that I could do well, especially as I hadn't done well in high school. I started getting A's in classes like math. That really boosted my self-esteem, especially when I realized I was earning those A's through hard work; no one was giving them to me. When I was ready to graduate, a friend told me about Smith College's Ada Comstock Scholars Program for non-traditional-age women whose education has been interrupted. I didn't think I was good enough to be among the best of the best women students in the country, plus only 60 are chosen each year from a few hundred applicants. Friends encouraged me to apply. My community college professors wrote me recommendations. I was accepted not only to Smith, but also to Mt. Holyoke College, Rutgers University, Lesley College, as well as to my local college, Richard Stockton College of New Jersey."

START THE TRANSFER PROCESS EARLY

If you know you'll want to continue for your bachelor's degree when you enroll in community college, then start investigating the transfer process your first semester. Why? Because you must be sure that the courses you take will be transferable to the four-year institution of your choice and that you start your transfer process in a timely manner so you get admitted when you plan to attend.

Edwin Roman, transfer and articulation advisor, Bronx Community College (New York) counsels, "Many students are confused about what degrees and coursework are most transferable. If you're getting an AAS in Accounting, you're training to be a bookkeeper and to go to work immediately. If you're getting an AS degree in Business with an accounting major, however, you're getting a degree and coursework that can be more easily transferred if you decide to go on. If you don't understand the difference, you can end up with the wrong degree and credits that aren't acceptable for transfer to a four-year institution. You may end up taking extra coursework and spending time and money that wouldn't have been necessary. Don't be afraid to ask for help in understanding the transfer process and how to plan so you're on the right track."

You also want to be sure that you can transfer the maximum number of credits so that you don't have to repeat coursework for which you have already paid at community college or take additional coursework to meet the four-year institution's requirements. You may want to take only a few courses at community college before transferring to a four-year institution, but you still want to be sure those credits transfer.

Get Expert Advice

Transferring can be complicated even when transfer or articulation agreements are in place between your community college and four-year institutions. If you enroll in a transfer degree program or you just want to transfer a few courses to a four-year institution, your best course of action is to speak with an advisor in your community college's transfer office *and* to a transfer advisor at the four-year institution that interests you. These advisors will be your best sources of information for helping you understand the transfer program and process.

Transfer advisors can help you

✓ Discover information about the transfer process at four-year institutions that interest you.

✓ Understand the academic requirements needed for a successful transfer.

✓ Develop a transfer plan of action to make sure you'll be on track with appropriate coursework.

✓ Gather information about the college's articulation agreements and others types of agreements with four-year institutions. It is helpful to read your community college's articulation agreement with the particular four-year college that you're interested in attending.

Transfer advisors can also tell you about other resources, such as:

✓ Transfer workshops and newsletters

✓ College transfer fairs, where you can speak to admissions offices from in-state and out-of-state four-year colleges and universities

✓ Visits organized by your college to local four-year institutions, as well as other college preview days or open houses

✓ Transfer guides or sheets that show transfer and admissions requirements for four-year institutions and their programs to help you plan your strategy and timetable for applying

✓ Electronic links to transfer offices of four-year institutions; plus print resources such as college catalogs, financial aid guides, college applications, and more

Your advisor can help you understand the requirements and map out a plan that will prepare you for a smooth transfer. Again, however, it's ultimately your responsibility to research and understand the transfer process and find out what will or will not transfer.

Remember, you will still need to apply and be admitted to the four-year college of your choice. With the right planning, you may be able to enter a four-year institution with junior standing or have advanced standing in a major or bachelor's degree program that interests you. You may still need to meet other requirements of the four-year institution or your major but you'll be ahead in terms of credits that will count toward your bachelor's degree.

Early on, when you know where you want to go, speak with the four-year institution's transfer advisor and check out the transfer information on their Web site. Joan Jagodnik, assistant director of community college relations at Portland State University (Oregon), observes, "It's helpful for students to speak not only with their community college advisors, but also to get advice from the four-year institution. In a sense, they can work *backwards* by first getting the general education, major, degree, and transfer requirements from the four-year institution and then matching up their program at community college to those requirements. There are lots of opportunities to meet with transfer advisors from four-year institutions. Three or four times a term, for example, we send advisors to community colleges in the area. Students can bring their transcripts to see if they are on track for transfer. Our office is also equipped with multiple resources for anyone who wants to come in to get advice about transferring."

> **TIP:** Some state education systems have online transfer information for their colleges and universities. These systems allow students and advisers to look up course equivalencies and courses recommended for specific majors, and sometimes to evaluate students' courses and grades to determine course equivalencies at transfer institutions. The Maryland ARTSYS (http://artweb.usmd.edu) shows recommended transfer programs for all Maryland public institutions and many private institutions. You can see what courses to take at a Maryland community college that will transfer smoothly into a specific major at a four-year institution. Check with your transfer office to see if an online system is available in your state.

Four-year institutions, especially those that have a high percentage of transfer students from community colleges, are very sensitive to your needs and concerns. Take advantage of their expertise and transfer office services. Their goal is to ease your transition to the college or university and to give you a point of contact on campus even *before* you become a student there.

CHECK OUT TRANSFER AGREEMENTS

You can transfer to any college that will accept you, but those that have transfer or articulation agreements with your community college will be the ones where it will be easiest to transfer credits because of this prior understanding. Articulation agreements often allow you to complete an associate's degree at community college and then transfer into the four-year college with standing as a junior. You'll want to check out your college's agreements with *both* in-state and out-of state colleges and universities so you'll know all the options available to you. These agreements can change, so be sure you've got the most recent information from your community college adviser, as well as from the four-year school.

It is a fact that community college students routinely transfer to four-year colleges and universities *with or without* articulation agreements between institutions. If no articulation agreement is in place between your community college and a four-year institution of interest to you, you can still plan to transfer by digging into the four-year college's catalog to identify general studies courses and courses in your major that might be a match for courses at your community college and that might transfer. This can be confusing so be sure to speak and work with your advisor and with a representative from the four-year college to make sure you can transfer as many credits as possible.

> **TIP:** A special type of transfer program, a dual admissions program, can help you complete a two-year degree in an eligible program of study at community college and guarantee your admission and transfer of credits to specific four-year colleges and universities. You may be eligible for a transfer scholarship, have access to the four-year institution's facilities, be able to take coursework at both your community college and the four-year school, plus have more opportunities for honors programs, internships, and study-abroad programs. As soon as you enroll in community college, check with your admissions or transfer office to see if your community college participates in a dual admissions program with a four-year institution, and to see if you're eligible to apply.

TIMELINE FOR TRANSFER—BY THE CREDIT

It's all in the timing. As mentioned earlier in this chapter, transferring is another one of those college processes where the earlier you start, the better off you are. The timeline below outlines steps for a successful transfer that you can begin taking as early as your first semester (quarter) at community college. This timeline assumes you are going to earn an associate's degree (about 60 semester credits or 90 quarter credits). You may decide to transfer *before* you complete a degree or certificate, but many of the steps outlined below will be helpful to you also.

Transfer Timeline by Credits

0–12 Semester Credits (0–18 Quarter Credits)

❏ Work closely with your advisor to plan your coursework to meet your academic goals and your transfer goals. If you know what major interests you, get a transfer guide for your major so that you can match your required coursework to that required by your transfer institution. (You don't need to have a major to transfer.)

❏ Start attending transfer workshops and transfer events.

❏ Start identifying four-year institutions that interest you, especially those with articulation agreements with your community college.

13–30 Semester Credits (19–44 Quarter Credits)

❏ Explore resources available to you for researching college transfer articulation agreements, and start contacting the transfer offices of four-year institutions.

❏ Begin to research colleges and universities that offer academic programs and activities that you want to pursue, and start contacting them for admissions guidelines, a catalog, financial aid, and all deadlines for housing, financial aid, and so on.

❏ See if there are any tests such as the SAT/ACT that you will need to take for the institutions that interest you. International students might need to take the TOEFL examination.

❏ Attend a College Transfer Fair and speak with a transfer advisor or arrange a meeting with an advisor at the four-year college to discuss your transfer goals and plans.

31–45 Semester Credits (45–74 Quarter Credits)

❏ Attend a transfer workshop and speak with an adviser at both community college and your proposed four-year institution, if you haven't already done so, to make sure you're on track for transferring credits!

❏ Start focusing on when you plan to graduate and when you plan to start classes at your transfer college. Speak to an academic advisor and be sure you're on track with required coursework for graduation.

❏ Focus in on those colleges where you plan to apply; email or phone the admissions office or transfer office with your questions. If you know your major, contact your prospective major department to see if there are specific departmental admission requirements.

❏ Get your application materials and know the application deadlines for the transfer college(s) where you are applying. Begin to complete and mail your applications (remember transcripts, letters of recommendation, and so on).

❏ Start researching financial aid and scholarship opportunities. Begin to apply for scholarships, *especially transfer scholarships*.

❏ Arrange for your community college transcripts to be sent, as well as those from any other college you have attended. High school transcripts might be necessary also.

46–61 Semester Credits (75–89 Quarter Credits)

❏ Make sure you're on track to graduate.

❏ Mail those applications if you haven't done so already!

❏ Remember: Financial aid is awarded on an academic year basis. Complete the FAFSA between January and March for the NEXT academic year. Check out the transfer college's deadlines for scholarships. Many deadlines will be in the fall of the year *before* you transfer.

❏ Wait to hear from colleges and either accept or reject their offers by the stated date (usually around May 1 for fall admittance).

Confirm your intention to enroll and submit any required deposit to the college or university of your choice.

❏ Have your transcript with your final grades sent to your transfer institution. Have your transcript evaluated by the four-year college for the number of credits that will transfer.

After Graduation (Usually 60+ Semester Credits or 90 Quarter Credits)

❏ Get ready to attend your new college or university. Be sure to attend an orientation for transfer students so you'll know the ropes at your new school.

❏ If you've *just* decided you'd like to transfer, see your community college transfer advisor *immediately*!

Stay Connected!

You'll find community college offers many opportunities to stay connected, whether it's simply through attending athletic and cultural events on campus, going back for some additional courses, or by participating in a campus-based association. Community college will be there at any stage of your education or career to help you accomplish another career, personal, or educational goal.

CONTINUE TO LEARN AND ENJOY THE CAMPUS

Community colleges are all about life-long learning, so you'll be able to re-connect with the college in whatever way you want to do so, whether you've just taken a few courses there or earned a certificate or degree.

You'll be welcomed to return to take that course that's of personal interest to you, such as photography or Spanish. Or you'll be able to add to your skills base by updating your computer skills or taking a quick course in how to set up a small business. If you've entered the profession of teaching, you might need continuing education credits to maintain your license.

You may find that the community college you attended will be a valuable partner in training employees for you through contracted programs designed to meet your special needs. Your community college can also help you stay current with changes in your field of expertise. At some point in your life, you may even want to change careers again. Community college can again give you that new start.

Of course, you will always find the college's door open to you and everyone in your family to take full advantage of its educational opportunities, services to the community, and facilities.

Join A Circle Of Alumni

Your community college alumni association is an excellent way for you to give your college a hand while maintaining contact with fellow students, faculty, and staff.

Jessica Warnick, director of the alumni association at Montgomery College (Maryland), says, "One of the biggest myths that community college alumni associations have to dispel for students is that someone isn't an alumnus because he or she didn't graduate or receive a degree from the college. Whether you just took a few courses, transferred to another college before earning your degree or certificate, or have taken continuing education or workforce development courses, you can still be a member of the alumni association."

You can choose the level of participation that is most comfortable for you. You may simply want to receive the college newsletter or participate occasionally in a special event such as a golf tournament. Or you might want to become a more active member who helps recruit new students, answers the phones at the annual phone-a-thon, or holds an official position with the association.

Bob Hydorn, current president of the Montgomery College Alumni Association and a 1971 graduate, has been actively involved for seven years with the association. He says, "Alumni are great ambassadors for the college and can do everything from working with local and state government officials to ensure adequate funding to talking to high school students about the benefits of attending community college to raising funds for

> **TIP:** Some alumni associations have chapters devoted to specific occupations such as nursing or engineering.

scholarships. Participating in the alumni association is an excellent way to give something back to the place where you got your start. And, it's exciting and gratifying to have a role in the growth and expansion of the college."

Whatever you decide to do, staying connected is easy. You'll receive some benefits from joining, and joining isn't expensive—in fact it's often free or there is a modest membership fee. Some member benefits that your alumni association may include are

- ✓ A free subscription to your college's alumni magazine, newspaper, or e-newsletter
- ✓ Invitations to special events, such as campus alumni day and alumni gatherings off campus
- ✓ Career-related services including resume and interview workshops or assistance, plus job search and placement
- ✓ Borrowing privileges at the campus library or libraries
- ✓ Reduced fees for use of college facilities such as a gym or a tennis court; special ticket prices for cultural, performing arts, or theatrical events; reduced rates on campus merchandise

Alumni associations typically recognize outstanding contributions to the college and community by their alumni. You could even receive an award as an Outstanding Alumnus! Or, your son or daughter could be eligible for a scholarship available from the alumni association.

> **FAST FACT:** Since 1982, through its Outstanding Alumni Award, the American Association of Community Colleges has recognized alumni who have excelled in their fields and given back to their communities. Recipients include film director, writer, and producer George Lucas, who attended Modesto Junior College, California. See www.aacc.nche.edu for the complete list of recipients.

Give Back!

If you have some time and want to help someone else get a start at college or in their career, there are a variety of ways you can show your appreciation to your college and help other students on their way.

Linda V. Siegmann says, "Your community college needs you to come back and tell your story to other students. I've done that several times. It's very rewarding for me to know that I've inspired other students, especially women like me—in their thirties with children—to know that they can do whatever they set their minds to. If you motivate even one person to go beyond what they think is their best, you've made a huge impact."

Here are some ways you can give back to your school.

✓ Be a mentor to a current student or a graduate, or help students make a career connection by serving on a Career Day panel or by giving informational job interviews to students interested in your field of employment.

✓ Serve on a community college advisory board or on a workforce development advisory board.

✓ Spread the word about community colleges and their advantages as a guest speaker at educational and civic associations and events.

✓ Make a donation to help your community college build its scholarship or endowment fund.

SNAPSHOT: Athena Lapan is a Jack Kent Cooke Scholar from Central Piedmont Community College (North Carolina) who now attends Johnson & Wales University. After attaining her goals of becoming an executive chef and opening her own restaurant, Athena wants to turn her talents to teaching in community college. She says, "I want to do for someone else what my teachers did for me—inspire, give self-confidence, build self-esteem. For me, giving is what community college is all about. The community gives you the opportunity to get an education. Your instructors and the college give you the opportunity to excel. Then, it's your turn to give back to the community in some way."

Reach for the Stars!

Now that you've come full circle with this book, you can see that community college can help change your life and enable you to reach for the stars. That's the inspiring message that the many people interviewed in this book are sending to you. They took a chance, bet on themselves, and accomplished their goals with the help of community college. You can, too.

Victor B. Smith, Sr. did. The former state corrections officer will soon graduate from Community College of Philadelphia. He'll enroll at Arcadia University (Pennsylvania) in their criminal justice program and hopes to go on for a master's degree. Romanian immigrant and journalist Marga C. Fripp did. Although she did not speak English when she first enrolled in Montgomery College (Maryland), she completed her associate's degree and is now studying in the communications program at the University of Maryland University College. Travis Huelsebusch did. He completed his aviation maintenance technology degree at Cincinnati State Technical and Community College, works full-time at a local airport, and has entered Embry-Riddle Aeronautical University.

Community college graduates can be found in all walks of life. Just browse through any community college alumni magazine or

> *"Community college and Smith College opened my eyes to possibilities I had never dreamed of. Taking each educational step was like jumping off a cliff without a parachute, but I survived and thrived. My education has had a ripple effect on other women in my family. I'm the first person in my family to go to college, but now one of my sisters has her master's degree in teaching and the other one is finishing college at age 53."*
> —Pamela Karwasinski, Atlantic County (now Cape) Community College (New Jersey)

Web site, and you'll see people of all ages, social, economic, and educational backgrounds, ethnicities, races, and nationalities whose lives were transformed by their experience at community college. They followed their dreams and have succeeded in all fields of endeavor—business, healthcare, architecture, law, film making, engineering, printing, design, politics, construction, automotive maintenance. You name the field; you'll find a community college alumnus there.

So, no matter what your dream is—earning a degree to start your career in nursing, becoming an electrician, getting your real estate license, becoming a lawyer, starting your own business, or simply getting your college degree—it's your dream. And community college is there to teach you, inspire you, and help you reach for the stars.

Community colleges change lives. Let one change yours.

Find Out More

+ *What Color is My Parachute?: A Practical Manual for Job-Hunters and Career-Changers* by Richard Bolles. (Ten Speed Press, 2006.) You'll find plenty of great advice at the companion Web site, www.jobhuntersbible.com.

+ www.monster.com is the best-known Internet-based employment resource with thousands of job postings each year. You can post your resumé here also.

+ *The Fiske Guide to Colleges* by Edward Fiske. (Sourcebooks, Inc.) Published annually. See also www.fiskeguide.com.

+ The National Articulation and Transfer Network (NATN) brings together over 200 urban high schools, community colleges, and four-year institutions to help students of color identify opportunities to further their education. Find out more about the network at www.natn.org. Its companion Web site, www.collegestepz.net, focuses on the transfer process, allows you to search for colleges to match your interests, and offers convenient links to financial aid and career information.

Notes

Chapter 1

1. Test Your Community College Knowledge

Question 2: U.S. Department of Education, National Center for Education Statistics. *Digest of Statistics.* (Washington, D.C.: U.S. Government Printing Office, 2004). Table 178: Total fall enrollment in degree-granting institutions, by attendance status, sex of student, and type and control of institution: Selected years, 1970 to 2002. www.nces.ed.gov.

Question 3: Philippe, Kent A., and Leila González Sullivan. *National Profile of Community Colleges: Trends and Statistics,* 4th edition. (Washington, D.C.: Community College Press, 2005), 1.

Question 4: McPhee, Sara. *Hot Programs at Community Colleges* [Research Brief]. (Washington, D.C.: American Association of Colleges, 2004), 2. Table 1: Top 15 Hot Programs For Credit and Noncredit Combined.

Question 5: Levinson, David L. *Community Colleges: A Reference Handbook.* (Santa Barbara: ABC-CLIO, Inc., 2005). 20–21.

2. Philippe and Sullivan (2005), 9. Table 12: Number of Community Colleges by State: 2004.

3. U.S. Department of Education, National Center for Educational Statistics. *The Condition of Education 2005.* NCES 2005-094. (Washington, D.C.: U.S. Government Printing Office, 2005). Table 7-1: Total undergraduate enrollment in degree-granting 2- and 4-year postsecondary institutions, by sex, attendance status, and type of institution, with projections: Fall 1970–2014. www.nces.ed.gov.

4. Philippe and Sullivan (2005), ix.

5. *The Condition of Education 2005.* Table 7-1: Total undergraduate enrollment in degree-granting 2- and 4-year postsecondary institutions, by sex, attendance status, and type of institution, with projections: Fall 1970–2014.

6. American Association of Community Colleges. www.aacc.nche.edu. (Click on About Community Colleges and then Historical Information); Phillippe and Sullivan (2005), 1–6.

7. Cohen, Arthur. M., and Florence B. Brawer. *The American Community College,* 4th edition. (San Francisco: Jossey-Bass, 2003), 24–26.

8. Saffian, Steven R. "Making Spaces: Two-Year Campus Residential Facilities." *Community College Journal,* 72, no. 5, April/May (2002), 43.

9. The College Board. *Trends in College Pricing, 2005.* (New York: The College Board, 2005), 5. www.collegeboard.com/prod_downloads/press/cost05/trends_college_pricing_05.pdf.

10. Hoachlander, Gary, Anna C. Siroka, and Laura Horn. "Community College Students: Goals, Academic Preparation, and Outcomes." *The Education Statistics Quarterly,* 5, no. 2 (2003). nces.ed.gov/programs/quarterly/vol_5/5_2/q4_1.asp. Topic: Postsecondary Education.

11. U.S. Census Bureau. *The Big Payoff: Educational Attainment and Synthetic Estimates of Work-Life Earnings.* (Washington, D.C.: U.S. Department of Commerce, 2002), 4. Figure 3: Educational Attainment and Synthetic Estimates of Work-Life Earnings. www.census.gov/prod/2002/pubs/p23-210.pdf.

Chapter 2

1. The University of Austin, Community College Leadership Program. *Community College Survey of Student Engagement: Engaging Students, Challenging the Odds.* (Austin, Texas, 2005). www.ccssee.org.

2. Adelman, Clifford. *Moving Into Town — and Moving On: The Community College in the Lives of Traditional Age Students.* (Washington, D.C.: U.S. Department of Education, 2005), xiii, 11.

3. Philippe, Kent A., and Leila González Sullivan. *National Profile of Community Colleges: Trends and Statistics,* 4th edition. (Washington, D.C.: Community College Press, 2005), 20.

4. U.S. Department of Education. National Center for Education Statistics. *Digest of Statistics, 2004.* (Washington, D.C.: U.S. Government Printing Office, 2004). Table 175: Total fall enrollment in degree-granting institutions by control and type of institution, and age and attendance status of students: 2001. www.nces.ed.gov.

5. Community College Population table

For gender and attendance status: Digest of Statistics, 2004. Table 178: Total fall enrollment in degree granting institutions, by attendance status, sex of student, and type and control of institution: Selected years, 1970 to 2002.

For work statistics: Phillippe and Sullivan (2005), 50. Table. 2.15: Employment Statistics of Public Community College Students by Attendance Status and Age: 2003–2004.

For race and ethnicity: U.S. Department of Education, National Center for Education Statistics. Integrated Postsecondary Education Data System. (Spring, 2003). Table 12: Enrollment in Title IV degree-granting institutions, by race/ethnicity, level of institution, control of institution, and student level: United States, Fall 2002. nces.ed.gov/das/library/ipeds_tab.asp.

6. Horn, Laura, Katharin Peter, and Kathryn Rooney. *Profile of Undergraduates in U.S. Postsecondary Institutions: 1999–2000.* National Center for Education Statistics, NCES 2000-168. (Washington, D.C.: U.S. Department of Education), 56. Table 1.6: Percentage of undergraduates attending postsecondary institutions in home state, the number of miles between home and postsecondary institutions, and percentage of undergraduates who ever attended community college.

7. Boggs, George R. "Community Colleges in a Perfect Storm," *Change: The Magazine of Higher Learning.* 36, no. 6 (November/December, 2004), 8.

Chapter 3

1. McPhee, Sara. *Hot Programs at Community Colleges* [Research Brief]. (Washington, D.C.: American Association of Colleges, 2004), 1. Figure 1: Top Five Fields of Study.

2. American Association of Community Colleges. www.aacc.nche.edu/Content/NavigationMenu/HotIssues/Homeland_Security/Homeland_Security.htm.

3. Hecker, Daniel E. "Occupational Employment Projections to 2014." *Monthly Labor Review* (November, 2005), 75. Table 2: Fastest-growing occupations 2004–2014.

4. U.S. Department of Labor. *Occupational Handbook 2006-07: Tomorrow's Jobs.* Table 1: Fastest growing occupations and occupations projected to have the largest numerical increases in employment between 2004–2014, by level of postsecondary education or training. www.bls.gov/oco/oco2003.htm.

5. U.S. Census Bureau. "Current Population Survey." *Annual Demographic Survey* (March Supplement. 2005). PINC-03: Educational Attainment — People 25 Years Old and Over, by Total Money Earnings in 2004, Work Experience in 2004, Age, Race, Hispanic Origin, and Sex. pubdb3.census.gov/macro/032005/perinc/new03_001.htm.

Chapter 4

Holmes, Natalie C. "One-on-One Connection Eases Entry for High School Students to Community College," *Community College Times*, XVII, no. 13 (June 21, 2005).

Chapter 5

1. www.collegeboard.com/highered/clep/examination.

Chapter 6

1. U.S. Department of Education, National Center for Education Statistics. *Postsecondary Institutions in the United States: Fall 2004 and Degrees and Other Awards Conferred 2003–2004.* (2005), 8. Table 4: Changes in academic year average price of attendance and components of price for full-time, first-time degree/certificate seeking undergraduates at Title IV [eligible for federal student aid] public institutions by level of institution, residency and student housing, United States, academic years 2001–2002 and 2004–2005.

2. College Board. *Trends in College Pricing 2005.* (NY: College Board, 2005), 17.

Chapter 7

1. Vaughn, George B. *The Community College Story,* 2nd edition. (Washington, D.C.: Community College Press, 2000), 17.

Chapter 8

1. Wyner, Joshua. "Educational Equity and the Transfer Student," *The Chronicle of Higher Education*, 52, no. 23 (February 10, 2006), B6.

2. Byrne, Joseph P. "Honors Programs in Community Colleges: A Review of Recent Issues and Literature," *Community College Review,* 26, no. 2 (Fall: 1998), 67.

Chapter 9

1. Prentice, Mary, Gail Robinson, and Sara McPhee. *Service Learning in Community Colleges: 2003 National Survey Results.* [Research Brief] (Washington, D.C.: American Association of Community Colleges, 2003), 1.

Chapter 10

1. Vaughn, George B. *The Community College Story*, 2nd edition. (Washington, D.C.: Community College Press, 2000), 9; Wyner, Joshua. "Educational Equity and the Transfer Student." *The Chronicle of Higher Education.* 52, no. 23 (February 10, 2006.), B6.

Talk the Talk:
Terms You Need to Know

Academic Advising   Help given while you are planning what courses you need to take and in what sequence to fulfill your academic goals and to meet requirements for a certificate, degree, and graduation. Academic advising is sometimes called academic counseling.

Academic Calendar   Important dates during the college year, such as registration deadlines, financial aid deadlines, and days the college is closed.

Academic Year   The annual period of time at college when classes are held.

Accreditation   The process by which an impartial organization does a thorough assessment of a college and its ability to provide appropriate faculty, curriculum, and facilities for students. An accredited college or program is one that has been certified as fulfilling certain standards set by a national or regional professional association.

Adjunct Faculty   A faculty member who teaches one or two courses at the college in a term and who is not considered to be employed full time by the college.

Articulation Agreement   An agreement between educational institutions that allows one institution to accept credits from another institution. The credits are transferred from one college to the other.

Assessment and Placement Test   Tests or other measurement instruments that determine which level of coursework is best suited to students' skills level. When you are first admitted to college, your basic skills (reading, writing, mathematics, English language) will be assessed to determine if you need to strengthen these skills before you enroll in college-level coursework. To identify potential majors or career interests, you may also take some tests at the career center to assess your interests.

Associate's Degree   A two-year degree from a college that prepares you to enter the workforce or to transfer to a four-year institution or university.

Associate in Applied Science (AAS)   The degree generally sought for a technological or other career program leading directly to employment. Students who earn this degree can also transfer to other colleges for a baccalaureate degree, but may be required to take additional coursework.

Associate in Arts Degree (AA)   A degree for those who plan to pursue baccalaureate or professional studies in fields such as the liberal arts, communications, education, the arts, or business.

Associate in Science Degree (AS)   A degree for students who plan to pursue baccalaureate studies in the natural, physical, or computer sciences, or to complete the first two years before transfer to a four-year institution.

Baccalaureate or Bachelor's Degree   A degree in a specific field offered by a four-year college or university.

Basic Skills Education   Coursework in subjects such as writing, reading, mathematics, English composition, and language designed to enhance your skills level so that you can take college-level coursework. Also referred to as developmental or remedial education.

Bursar   The person who is responsible for collecting tuition and fees.

Career Program   A curriculum designed primarily for direct entry into the workplace upon completion, although some programs also enable you to transfer to a four-year institution.

Catalog   A handbook that includes information about the academic calendar, tuition and fees, degree and certificate programs, and requirements that you will need to fulfill.

Certificate   A record of successful completion of a short program of study (often a year or less if you attend full time, typically 12–38 credit hours), designed to prepare you for immediate entry into the workforce.

Continuing Education   (sometimes called community education) The department at the college that is in charge of non-credit courses to expand adults' job skills, basic skills, or language skills. Sometimes non-credit workforce development programs are also included under the Continuing Education Department. Other times, workforce development is a separate department and may refer to both for-credit and non-credit coursework intended to improve job skills, or to coursework designed for specific businesses and their employees.

Cooperative Education   A form of study in which you alternate classroom study and a paid work experience related to your major.

Co-Requisite   A requirement that a course must be taken during the same semester (quarter) as another course.

Cost of Attendance   The total amount it will cost students to go to school—usually expressed as a yearly figure. It is determined using rules established by law. The COA includes tuition and fees; on-campus room and board (or a housing and food allowance for off-campus students); and allowances for books, supplies, transportation, loan fees, and, if applicable, dependent care. It also includes miscellaneous expenses, including an allowance for the rental or purchase of a personal computer. Costs related to a disability are also covered. The COA includes reasonable costs for eligible study-abroad programs as well. For students attending less than half time, the COA includes only tuition and fees and an allowance for books, supplies, transportation, and dependent-care expenses.

Counseling   A general term that refers to guidance and assistance you receive from various student service offices on campus. For example, you may go to the career center for counseling about your choice of major or future job. You may need personal counseling to help you with individual or family problems affecting your studies. You may receive counseling about the transfer process from the transfer center. Some colleges put all counseling services under one department; others have separate centers for various types of counseling activities.

Credit Courses   Students earn credits, a unit of value, for coursework that counts toward their degree. Usually, credit courses have certain requirements for coursework, attendance, and/or laboratory work. Each course is worth a certain number of credits. The number of credits assigned to a course usually reflects the number of hours you spend in that class each week. If a class is worth three credits, it usually meets for three hours per week. See also Non-Credit Courses.

Curriculum   Your program of study; a set of required and elective courses designed to meet specific career or transfer goals and leading to a degree or a certificate upon successful completion. The word can also refer to all the courses that a college offers.

Default   Failure to keep your written promise to repay a loan.

Degree   Official confirmation by your college that you have successfully completed your program of studies. A two-year program in Arts, Science, and Applied Sciences leads to an associate's degree; a traditional four-year undergraduate program leads to the baccalaureate or bachelor's degree.

Developmental or Remedial Education   Basic skills courses such as reading, writing, and mathematics that often must be passed before a student can enroll in college-level courses. Also referred to as basic skills education.

Direct Loan (DL) Program   A student loan program administered by the U.S. Department of Education. Participating schools allow their students to borrow directly from the federal government instead of from a private lender.

Disbursement   The release and payment of loan funds by a lender.

Discipline   A particular subject that you are studying, such as biology or English.

Distance learning   Education that takes place between instructors and students outside the regular classroom, usually by electronic means, such as the Internet, televised courses, or video cassettes.

Electives   Classes that a student may choose to take, but which are not required to fulfill a particular curriculum.

Enrollment   The process by which someone becomes a student at a college. It usually includes application, assessment and placement testing, orientation, counseling, and registration for classes. You are enrolled as a full-time or part-time student depending on the number of courses or credits you take.

Expected Family Contribution (EFC)   The dollar amount that a family is expected to pay toward a student's educational costs. This federal calculation is based on factors such as family earnings, assets, students in college, and size of family.

Faculty   The academic staff of the college, that is, individuals with specific academic credentials and/or experience who are hired by the college to plan and teach courses. Full-time faculty have other responsibilities such as advising, participation in college committees, and sponsoring student clubs. Part-time faculty or adjuncts plan and teach one or two courses a semester and usually do not have additional responsibilities.

Federal Family Education Loan Program (FFEL)   Private lenders provide federally supported loans through this program.

Fees   Money charged by the college for specific services such as instruction (tuition), books, health services, use of facilities, and so on.

Financial Aid   Funds received by eligible students to assist them with the costs of attending college. Financial aid may come from many sources such as the federal government, state government, private lenders, or the college. Loans, scholarships, grants, and work-study programs are common forms of financial aid.

Financial Aid Package   The total amount of financial aid (federal and nonfederal) a student receives.

Free Application for Federal Student Aid (FAFSA)   The free federal application form students must first complete in order to apply for almost all forms of financial aid.

Full-Time Student   Generally, a student who is enrolled in at least 12 credit hours of coursework each semester.

General Educational Development (GED) Test   A series of five tests that students without a high school diploma may take to qualify for a high school equivalency certificate.

General Education Requirements   A core of required courses that students in both vocational/technical and transfer programs take for a well-rounded educational experience.

Grace Period   The period before loan payments must begin after a student either graduates, leaves school (unofficially or officially), or drops below half-time enrollment.

Grade   The value assigned to a student's academic performance, usually beginning with an "A" as the highest grade and ending with an "F" as the lowest. Grades are usually assigned a quality point or unit value. An "A" is usually worth 4 points, a "B" 3 points, a "C" 2 points, a "D" 1 point, and an "F" 0 points.

Grade Point Average   Also called the GPA, it is the average of all the grades received in courses. You multiply the point value of your grade (such as 4.0 points for an A) in each course by the number of credits per course, add all the points together, and divide by the total number of credits taken to determine your GPA. For example, if you take 3 courses, each worth three credits, and you receive an "A" (4.0) in each course, your GPA would be 4.0. (3 credits/course x 4 points = 12 total points/course x 3 courses = 36 total points divided by 9 credits = 4.0).

Grant A type of financial aid based usually on financial need, school cost, and enrollment status. Grants normally do not need to be repaid.

Guarantor The agency or institution that repays lenders in the event a student defaults (fails to pay) on a loan.

Internship Usually an unpaid work experience related to your major or an area of study that interests you.

Lender The institution that provides the money to be borrowed through the student loan program or a private loan.

Liberal Arts College studies that are intended to provide general knowledge and intellectual skills. Subjects such as fine arts, literature, humanities (art, English, foreign languages, music, philosophy), and natural and social sciences are grouped under the general term "liberal arts."

Loan Money that you borrow that must be repaid with interest, that is, the amount of money charged to borrow money.

Lower Division Courses offered for credit during the freshman (first) and sophomore (second) year. Students who are freshmen or sophomores are called lower-division students. Community colleges usually only teach lower-division courses.

Major A program of study selected as a student's primary area of study leading to the degree. Usually, you receive a degree in your major. For example, if you study English as your major, you will graduate with an Associate of Arts degree in English.

Minor   A field of study that is secondary to your primary field of study or major.

Non-Credit Courses   A type of class for which no college credit is earned toward a certificate or degree. Non-credit classes generally do not contribute to your grade point average or count toward your degree.

Part-Time Student   A student who is enrolled in less than 12 credit hours per semester.

Pell Grant   A federal government grant based on financial need awarded to undergraduate students who have not earned a bachelor's or professional degree. Unlike a loan, a Pell grant does not need to be repaid.

Perkins Loan   A federal loan offered by some schools to provide the neediest students with low-interest loans.

PLUS Loan   A loan made to qualifying parents of dependent undergraduate students, available through the federal government's Direct Loan Program and Federal Family Education Loan Program (FFEL).

Post-Secondary Education   Any education that occurs beyond high school.

Prerequisite   A requirement that a certain course or courses must be successfully completed before you may enroll in some other course.

Probation   A status that describes students who do not make satisfactory academic progress.

Promissory Note   The legal and binding contract signed between the lender and the borrower, which states that the borrower will repay the loan as agreed upon in the terms of the contract.

Quarter   One type of term within an academic year, marking the beginning and end of classes. Each quarter is about 10–11 weeks in length. There are three quarters per academic year: fall, winter, and spring. Summer term is usually 4–11 weeks. One quarter credit = .667 semester credits.

Registration   The process by which you select, schedule, and enroll in courses for the semester or quarter.

Resumé   A document that outlines your educational and work experience plus contact information. It is usually written to apply for jobs.

Scholarship   An award that does not usually have to be paid back. It is based on merit, such as academic achievement or athletic skill, financial need, or other qualifications.

Semester   One type of academic term within an academic year, marking the beginning and end of classes. Each semester is 14–18 weeks in length and there are two semesters (fall and spring) in an academic year. 1 semester credit = 1.5 quarter credits.

Service Learning   A form of for-credit study that integrates service to the community with classroom learning to help you better understand the course content and learn about community issues.

Stafford Loan   A federal loan made available to students through the Direct Loan Program and the Federal Family Education Loan Program (FFEL).

State Grant Program   State funding coordinated by the state agency that provides grants to needy state residents who meet the eligibility criteria and who are pursuing post-secondary education.

Student Aid Report (SAR)   The SAR summarizes the information reported on the FAFSA. The schools students listed on the application receive electronic copies of the SAR and use the information to determine a student's eligibility for federal financial aid.

Student Handbook   A book that outlines students' rights and responsibilities, as well as the college's code of conduct.

Subsidized Loan   A loan on which the federal government pays the interest until you are required to begin repayment.

Syllabus   An overview of a course, prepared by an instructor and giving assignments, required reading, and the instructor's policies on attendance, grading, and other issues.

Transcript   A formal record of courses that a student has taken at high school or college and any diplomas, certificates or degrees completed. Transcripts usually show your grade, courses completed or attempted, and your grade point average. This is your official record of your academic career at an institution.

Transfer   The process of a student moving from one college to another; it also refers to the process of moving your credits from one college to another. A transfer student is one who intends to or does move from one college to another. Transferring requires a new application and admission to the new school.

Transfer Program   A two-year curriculum that is specifically designed to be the first half of a bachelor's degree program and to prepare you to transfer from community college to a four-year institution with a minimal loss of credits.

Tuition   The fee you pay at college that covers the cost of instruction. It is often based on the number of credit hours you take each academic period; some colleges charge a flat tuition rate for each semester or quarter.

Undergraduate   A student who is enrolled in college, but who has not yet completed a baccalaureate degree.

Unsubsidized Loan   A loan that you are responsible for paying from the date you receive the funds until it is paid completely, regardless of your enrollment status. Interest begins to accrue immediately on this type of loan.

Upper Division   Coursework that is offered for credit in the junior and senior years of study. Students who are juniors and seniors are also called upper division students.

Vocational/Technical Program A program to prepare you for a career or profession that is related to a specific trade, occupation, or vocation. If you specialize in a field of technology, such as computer science, the term "technical program" may be used.

Withdrawal A decision to remove yourself from the class roster for a course or a semester (quarter) because you are unable or unwilling to complete the coursework.

Work-Study Program A form of financial aid through the federal government by which eligible students are paid for part-time work on campus or community-based work while attending classes. Work study can also be used as a general term to refer to any combination of paid or unpaid work and coursework.

Index